THE BEAR

Originally published as
The Grizzly King

PRAISE FOR THE NOVEL

"The story of an orphaned baby bear and a huge adult male grizzly as they form a bond and flee the guns and dogs of two hunters is both suspenseful and highly emotional.... The climax, based on Curwood's experience, is a heart-stopper."
—Baton Rouge (LA) State Advocate

"Curwood's long-forgotten novel turns out to be thrilling.... The giant grizzly Thor finds himself pursued by a creature who has wounded him.... A cub whose mother has died licks the older bear's wounds and is allowed to follow him about.... The reader also follows Jim Langdon, a naturalist-hunter-writer, and Bruce Otto, a grizzled old hunter who knows all about bears. The time comes when Thor corners Jim Langdon...and man and bear are face to face. Spellbinding."
—Kirkus Reviews

"Curwood's stirring wilderness tale [is] a work by an ardent American conservationist and cult adventure writer."
—ALA Booklist

THE BEAR

A NOVEL

Originally published as
The Grizzly King

JAMES OLIVER CURWOOD

*Introduction by
Jean-Jacques Annaud*

NEWMARKET PRESS   NEW YORK

The Grizzly King copyright 1916 by James Oliver Curwood
Copyright renewed 1943 by Ethel M. Curwood
The Bear: A Novel, the movie tie-in expanded edition
of *The Grizzly King*, copyright © 1989 by Newmarket Press

The original text of *The Grizzly King* has been updated
to reflect current spelling usage.

Photographs copyright © 1989 Tri-Star Pictures.
Photographs taken during the shoot of *The Bear*
by Marianne Rosenstiehl.

This book published simultaneously in
the United States of America and in Canada.

The publisher wishes to acknowledge the estate of James Oliver Curwood, Columbia and Tri-Star Pictures, Renn Productions, and Jean-
Jacques Annaud for their cooperation in the publication of this book.

92 93 94   10 9 8 7 6 5 4 3

Library of Congress Cataloging-in-Publication Data
Curwood, James Oliver, 1878–1927.
The bear : a novel / by James Oliver Curwood.
p. cm.
Originally published under title: The grizzly king. 1916.
ISBN 1-55704-054-0 (hardcover)
ISBN 1-55704-131-8 (Medallion paperback)
1. Bears—Fiction. I. Curwood, James Oliver, 1878–1927.
Grizzly king.   II. Title.
PS3505.U92B4   1989   89-13247
813'.52—dc20   CIP

QUANTITY PURCHASES

Companies, professional groups, clubs, and other organizations
may qualify for special terms when ordering quantities of this title.
For information contact: Special Sales Dept., Newmarket Press,
18 East 48th Street, New York, N.Y. 10017, or call (212) 832-3575.

Book design by M. J. DiMassi
Manufactured in the United States of America

PUBLISHER'S NOTE

I take particular pleasure in bringing to your attention this book, which I believe is a long-lost American classic. Although it's been out of print on this continent for more than fifty years, in France the 1952 Hachette translation still sells well today.

The author is American—Michigan-born James Oliver Curwood. He wrote thirty-three books before he died at the age of forty-nine in 1927. This novel, originally published under the title *The Grizzly King*, is the basis for the feature film *The Bear*, which will dramatically acquaint a new generation of American readers with Curwood's story.

In his original 1916 preface, Curwood wrote: "I offer this [book with] a confession, and a hope; the confession of one who for years hunted and killed before he learned that the wild offered a more thrilling sport than slaughter— and the hope that what I have written may make others feel and understand that the greatest thrill of the hunt is not in killing, but in letting live."

Now, seventy-six years later, in an era when his message has far more meaning than ever before, thanks to director Jean-Jacques Annaud's extraordinary film and to this re-publication Curwood's hope may be fulfilled beyond his wildest dreams.

ESTHER MARGOLIS,
President and Publisher,
Newmarket Press, New York City
Spring, 1992

Introduction

I began to dream of making *The Bear,* and so learned about
James Oliver Curwood's wonderful book *The Grizzly King,*
because as a filmmaker I am interested in portraying our
most basic and timeless emotions. After I made *Quest for
Fire,* which is a movie about the complex emotions felt by
primeval people, I wanted to look even deeper, to explore
to its roots our emotional behavior. As I read all I could
find on ethology—the study of animal behavior—I began to realize I was reading about myself. This was
human comedy in the animal kingdom! I immediately
wanted to use this extraordinary material to explore myself
and my own species and to show that we are not as unique
as we might think. I thought: Why, for example, don't we
show an animal in love? Then we would see how similar
we really are and how much we can sympathize with one
another.

So I had in mind a movie—not a documentary, but an
emotional drama—in which animals would be the stars and
the audience would share their joys and pains as they would
those of human characters in any other work. All I needed
was a story. Then one day my friend Gérard Brach, who
became the screenwriter for *The Bear,* showed me *Le Grizzly,*

the French translation of James Oliver Curwood's novel, which he had won as a child in a school contest and which he remembered fondly. I read it in a single afternoon, and that was it. I was amazed! I knew I had found exactly what I was looking for.

The Grizzly King is the adventure of two bears and the men who hunt them in the spectacular, fearsome wilderness of nineteenth-century British Columbia. But it is also much, much more. Curwood's greatest gift to us is his remarkable imagination and insight into animals—their emotions and habits, their personalities and environs. In this book he uses this vision to craft a beautifully moving drama about a full range of emotions that we are used to thinking of as human and describe that way, but that are, in fact, universal—including love (maternal care and mating bonds), loneliness (the insecurity of a cub), sympathy (the nurturing of young), pride (territorial dominance), and, most important, forgiveness (selective aggression).

This book is extraordinary if only because Curwood is a marvelous storyteller who creates wonderful characters. From the moment we meet Thor, the mighty bear, the king of the forest, we are both in awe of his power and charmed by his earnestness and honesty. He is a dignified ruler, but he is not above scratching his back on trees, wallowing in the mud, and being grouchy or lazy or playful.

Thor is the real hero of this story, and his reactions to the hunters lie at the heart of Curwood's message. To say too much would be to reveal the novel's beautiful secret. But it is important to note that Curwood refrains from giving Thor overly moralistic or "human" motivations. Thor remains a bear—he acts out of instinct—but one with a whimsical, essentially sympathetic personality.

The hunters burst into Thor's world and immediately turn it upside down, but in the end even Jim Langdon, an enthusiastic hunter, finds room for compassion. It is through Langdon's eyes that Curwood tells the story of his own transformation from a hunter to a friend of bears. Curiously, Bruce Otto—the wise trapper and guide—is the story's least sympathetic character, but it is his inflexibility and hard-shelled outlook that make him so important. He is the bear's worst enemy, but we recognize and identify with him.

By the time Curwood introduces you to the cub Muskwa—whom Thor begrudgingly adopts and takes under his wing—you will already be thoroughly engrossed in this story. But this little bear will knock you off your feet all over again. I identified with Muskwa immediately and decided that I wanted to retell the story through his eyes because his emotions are so basic and so universal: he is a baby who has lost his mother and needs protection; he feels a natural concern for the wounded Thor. His coming of age is a truly moving process.

Curwood paints all these pictures with such sensitivity and such a thorough knowledge of his subjects that they came alive for me at once and left raw emotions and spectacular images which stayed with me long after I'd finished the book. In making *The Bear* I wanted to have the same startling impact as Curwood achieved in *The Grizzly King*.

But projecting all this onto a movie screen was to be no easy matter. In fact, it required years of planning the details of every scene, of scouting the world's most remote mountains for the appropriate location, of casting stars and stand-ins among hundreds of bears, and of then training these bears. Dozens of skilled, dedicated people—from animal trainers to animation artists—were involved. We spent six months in the Dolomite Mountains, often waiting through days of rain and bear stubbornness to capture a few seconds on film. In the end we shot over a million feet of film at frightening costs.

But the most important and memorable aspect of the entire project for me was getting to know the bears. I was totally unprepared to like them as much as I did. In fact, even after reading the book, I wasn't sure whether to use bears as the characters. After all, Curwood's story is universal enough to be about practically any mammal, and bears—these enormous, stubborn, frighteningly powerful creatures—are not the easiest to work with. So I went casting at the zoo and looked at wolves, tigers, elephants, apes; none of them were quite right. When I got to the bears, I saw immediately that this animal had something exceptional. Of course it is brutal, menacing, dangerous—it's a killer! But it is also an animal that we find it easy to identify with. Bears can stand on two legs and use their arms. Their claws look like fingers. Their entire bone structure is very similar to ours, as is their vocal system (actually, in the first few months, the cubs sound almost exactly like human children). So I knew they were perfect because they are undeniably beasts—as big and fierce as the wilderness itself— but at the same time they are often very expressive in ways we can understand.

This is not to say that they act like people. This story *is* fiction, but the fact is that, unlike actors, bears are unwilling and unable to be anything but bears. They do only what they feel. Nevertheless, so many times while shooting this movie, the entire film crew found itself transfixed, choked with emotion, on seeing the animals magically reinvent what was hoped for in the script. There was no need to impose human behavior on animals, for—and this is the entire point of the story—in these situations, humans would act the same way. *The Bear* shows us the animal within ourselves.

I began this project with the goal of discovering what kind of animal I am, of broadening my understanding of my instincts, my body, my emotions, my nature. James Oliver Curwood helped to set me on the right path, and working with bears on the film really transformed me. In retrospect, I used to see animals as almost like mechanical toys—each bear or wolf or tiger identical to the next and capable of only one response to a given situation. Now I understand the magnitude of my mistake. I now know that bears have personalities, as we do, and have feelings. I can't begin to describe, for example, the level of affection, tenderness, and mutual passion I witnessed between a mother bear and her cub. Watching such things, I have learned that despite all our culture and technology, on an emotional level there is not very much to distinguish us from animals. And I am happy and proud about this. I now understand better what our effort was and what the size of our success is.

Curwood's experiences in British Columbia had a very similar effect on him. He hunted bears for years until he had observed them enough to understand that they deserved the respect and affection they give to each other. I was very touched by the fact that he wrote this book for his son, so that he would not indulge, in Curwood's words, in "the lust for slaughter." "The greatest thrill of the hunt is not in killing," he wrote, "but in letting live."

I also greatly admired the fact that he came to such conclusions at a time when there were tens of thousands of bears and tens of thousands of miles of real wilderness in the world. Preserving wild animals and their habitat was of little concern to anyone. Now bears are disappearing rapidly all over the world. In France we have only sixteen unfortunate bears barely surviving in the wilderness. In America they survive in only a few states. And the vast areas of wilderness they need to survive are even more scarce. It is ironic that to shoot the last scene of the movie, which shows miles and miles of snowy landscape, we had to go to the Mackenzie Mountains in the Canadian Northwest Territories to find an area of that size, with no roads, no telephone wires, no fences, no pipelines.

Like Curwood, I hope my film, and the reissue of this

book, will have at least some impact on this sad situation. This is not, admittedly, my primary motivation. I am a filmmaker; my job is to entertain, to portray emotions, and to tell a story with images on a screen. But I have come to love and to need wilderness, and I want my daughter to be able to spend, as I did to make this movie, eight months of her life in areas with no planes or telephones or pollution, just forest and fresh water and wild animals. Any part I can play in saving that for her I am proud and happy to play.

Some progress, I am happy to report, has already been made. In France, because of the film, President François Mitterrand is fighting to protect the sixteen wild bears we have in the Pyrenees. In Austria and in Switzerland, because of the film, they are now trying to introduce bears and to create national parks for them. Also in Austria, they are thinking of canceling a huge hydroelectric dam scheduled to be built in a beautiful valley. In Finland, after seeing the film, people realized there was no law to protect bears from hunters, and they are now trying to enact such a law. Britain's Prince Charles, the king of Norway, and the queen of the Netherlands all attended screenings of the film as members of the World Wildlife Fund, and in each country there is now renewed interest in the welfare of bears.

These developments are very encouraging, and I am pleased to be a part of them. I feel that this book and the movie which grew out of it present an opportunity for bears to get the respect, the protection, and, perhaps most important, the territory they need in order to survive. Bears are rarely killed by hunters anymore. More often they die because, without ample room to forage and stake out their territory, they are too disoriented to eat and reproduce as they normally would. Everyone loves bears, but people either own the land they need or flock to the land set aside for them. If we truly love the bear, we must leave him alone.

So read this book and enjoy it. May it open your heart and mind as it did mine, and as it shows James Oliver Curwood's were opened more than seventy years ago.

JEAN-JACQUES ANNAUD*
Paris, France
August, 1989

*The Jean-Jacques Annaud production of *The Bear* opened in Paris on October 19, 1988, and during the next month in twelve other European countries. By August 1989, it had grossed $100 million and smashed virtually every box-office record, ranking it as one of the most successful films ever released, even before its opening in North America, the United Kingdom, Japan, and other countries. The story of the $22 million production is related in the book *The Odyssey of The Bear: The Making of the Film by Jean-Jacques Annaud*, published by Newmarket Press.

THE BEAR

A NOVEL

Originally published as
The Grizzly King

TO
MY BOY

PREFACE

IT IS with something like a confession that I offer this second of my nature books to the public—a confession, and a hope; the confession of one who for years hunted and killed before he learned that the wild offered a more thrilling sport than slaughter—and the hope that what I have written may make others feel and understand that the greatest thrill of the hunt is not in killing, but in letting live. It is true that in the great open spaces one must kill to live; one must have meat, and meat is life. But killing for food is not the lust of slaughter; it is not the lust which always recalls to me that day in the British Columbia mountains when, in less than two hours, I killed four grizzlies on a mountain slide—a destruction of possibly a hundred and twenty years of life in a hundred and twenty minutes. And that is only one instance of many in which I now regard myself as having been almost a criminal—for killing for the excitement of killing can be little less than murder. In their small

3

way my animal books are the reparation I am now striving to make, and it has been my earnest desire to make them not only of romantic interest, but reliable in their fact. As in human life, there are tragedy, and humor, and pathos in the life of the wild; there are facts of tremendous interest, real happenings and real lives to be written about, and very small necessity for one to draw on imagination. In *Kazan* I tried to give the reader a picture of my years of experience among the wild sledge dogs of the North. In *The Grizzly King* I have scrupulously adhered to facts as I have found them in the lives of the wild creatures of which I have written. Little Muskwa was with me all that summer and autumn in the Canadian Rockies. Pipoonaskoos is buried in the Firepan Range country, with a slab over his head, just like a white man. The two grizzly cubs we dug out on the Athabasca are dead. And Thor still lives, for his range is in a country where no hunters go—and when at last the opportunity came we did not kill him. This year (in July of 1916) I am going back into the country of Thor and Muskwa. I think I would know Thor if I saw him again, for he was a monster full-grown. But in two years Muskwa had grown from cubhood into full bearhood. And yet I believe that Muskwa would know *me* should we chance to meet again. I like to think that he has not forgotten the sugar, and the scores of times he cuddled up close to me at night, and the hunts we had together after roots and berries, and the sham fights with which we amused ourselves so often in camp. But, after all, perhaps he would not forgive me for that last day

4

when we ran away from him so hard—leaving him alone to his freedom in the mountains.

JAMES OLIVER CURWOOD
Owosso, Michigan
May 5, 1916

CHAPTER
ONE

WITH the silence and immobility of a great reddish-tinted rock, Thor stood for many minutes looking out over his domain. He could not see far, for, like all grizzlies, his eyes were small and far apart, and his vision was bad. At a distance of a third or a half a mile he could make out a goat or a mountain sheep, but beyond that his world was a vast sun-filled or night-darkened mystery through which he ranged mostly by the guidance of sound and smell.

It was the sense of smell that held him still and motionless now. Up out of the valley a scent had come to his nostrils that he had never smelled before. It was something that did not belong there, and it stirred him strangely. Vainly his slow-working brute mind struggled to comprehend it. It was not caribou, for he had killed many caribou; it was not goat; it was not sheep; and it was not the smell of the fat and lazy whistlers sunning themselves on the rocks, for he had eaten hundreds of whistlers. It was a scent that did not enrage him, and neither did it frighten him. He was curious, and yet he did not go down to seek it out. Caution held him back.

If Thor could have seen distinctly for a mile, or two miles, his eyes would have discovered even less than the wind brought to him from down the valley. He stood at the edge of a little plain, with the valley an eighth of a mile below him, and the break over which he had come that afternoon an eighth of a mile above him. The plain was very much like a cup, perhaps an acre in extent, in the green slope of the mountain. It was covered with rich, soft grass and June flowers, mountain violets and patches of forget-me-nots, and wild asters and hyacinths, and in the center of it was a fifty-foot spatter of soft mud which Thor visited frequently when his feet became rock-sore. To the east and the west and the north of him spread out the wonderful panorama of the Canadian Rockies, softened in the golden sunshine of a June afternoon.

From up and down the valley, from the breaks between the peaks, and from the little gullies cleft in shale and rock that crept up to the snow-lines came a soft and droning murmur. It was the music of running water. That music was always in the air, for the rivers, the creeks, and the tiny streams gushing down from the snow that lay eternally up near the clouds were never still.

There were sweet perfumes as well as music in the air. June and July—the last of spring and the first of summer in the northern mountains—were commingling. The earth was bursting with green; the early flowers were turning the sunny slopes into colored splashes of red and white and purple, and everything that had life was singing—the fat whistlers on their rocks, the pompous little gophers on their mounds, the big bumblebees that buzzed from flower to flower, the hawks in the valley, and the eagles over the peaks. Even Thor was singing in his way, for as he had paddled through the soft mud a few minutes before he had rumbled curiously deep down in his great chest. It was not a growl or a roar or a snarl; it was the noise he made when he was contented. It was his song.

And now, for some mysterious reason, there had suddenly come a change in this wonderful day for him. Motionless he still sniffed the wind. It puzzled him. It disquieted him without alarming him. To the new and strange smell that was in the air he was as keenly sensitive as a child's tongue to the first sharp touch of a drop of brandy. And then, at last, a low and sullen growl came like a distant roll of thunder from out of his chest. He was overlord of these domains, and slowly his brain told him that there should be no smell which he could not comprehend, and of which he was not the master.

Thor reared up slowly, until the whole nine feet of him rested on his haunches, and he sat like a trained dog, with his great forefeet, heavy with mud, drooping in front of his chest. For ten years he had lived in these mountains and never had he smelled that smell. He defied it. He waited for it, while it came stronger and nearer. He did not hide himself. Cleancut and unafraid, he stood up.

He was a monster in size, and his new June coat

shone a golden brown in the sun. His forearms were almost as large as a man's body; the three largest of his five knifelike claws were five and a half inches long; in the mud his feet had left tracks that were fifteen inches from tip to tip. He was fat, and sleek, and powerful. His eyes, no larger than hickory nuts, were eight inches apart. His two upper fangs, sharp as stiletto points, were as long as a man's thumb, and between his great jaws he could crush the neck of a caribou.

Thor's life had been free of the presence of man, and he was not ugly. Like most grizzlies, he did not kill for the pleasure of killing. Out of a herd he would take one caribou, and he would eat that caribou to the marrow in the last bone. He was a peaceful king. He had one law: "Let me alone!" he said, and the voice of that law was in his attitude as he sat on his haunches sniffing the strange smell.

In his massive strength, in his aloneness and his supremacy, the great bear was like the mountains, unrivaled in the valleys as they were in the skies. With the mountains, he had come down out of the ages. He was part of them. The history of his race had begun and was dying among them, and they were alike in many ways. Until this day he could not remember when anything had come to question his might and his right—except those of his own kind. With such rivals he had fought fairly and more than once to the death. He was ready to fight again, if it came to a question of sovereignty over the ranges which he claimed as his own. Until he was beaten he was dominator, arbiter, and despot, if he chose to be. He was dynast of the rich valleys and the green slopes, and liege lord of all living things about him. He had won and kept these things openly, without strategy or treachery. He was hated and he was feared, but he was without hatred or fear of his own—and he was honest. Therefore he waited openly for the strange thing that was coming to him from down the valley.

As he sat on his haunches, questioning the air with his keen brown nose, something within him was reaching back into dim and bygone generations. Never before had he caught the taint that was in his nostrils, yet now that it came to him it did not seem altogether new. He could not place it. He could not picture it. Yet he knew that it was a menace and a threat.

For ten minutes he sat like a carven thing on his haunches. Then the wind shifted, and the scent grew less and less, until it was gone altogether.

Thor's flat ears lifted a little. He turned his huge head slowly so that his eyes took in the green slope and the tiny plain. He easily forgot the smell now that the air was clear and sweet again. He dropped on his four feet, and resumed his gopher-hunting.

There was something of humor in his hunt. Thor weighed a thousand pounds; a mountain gopher is six inches long and weighs six ounces. Yet Thor would dig energetically for an hour, and rejoice at the end by swallowing the fat little gopher like a pill; it was his *bonne bouche*, the luscious tidbit in the quest of which he spent a third of his spring and summer digging.

He found a hole located to his satisfaction and began throwing out the earth like a huge dog after a rat. He was on the crest of the slope. Once or twice during the next half-hour he lifted his head, but he was no longer disturbed by the strange smell that had come to him with the wind.

CHAPTER
TWO

A MILE down the valley Jim Langdon stopped his horse where the spruce and balsam timber thinned out at the mouth of a coulee, looked ahead of him for a breathless moment or two, and then with an audible gasp of pleasure swung his right leg over so that his knee crooked restfully about the horn of his saddle, and waited.

Two or three hundred yards behind him, still buried in the timber, Otto was having trouble with Dishpan, a contumacious pack-mare. Langdon grinned happily as he listened to the other's vociferations, which threatened Dishpan with every known form of torture and punishment, from instant disembowelment to the more merciful end of losing her brain through the medium of a club. He grinned because Otto's vocabulary descriptive of terrible things always impending over the heads of his sleek and utterly heedless packhorses was one of his chief joys. He knew that if Dishpan should elect to turn somersaults while diamond-hitched under her pack, big, good-natured

Bruce Otto would do nothing more than make the welkin ring with his terrible, bloodcurdling protest.

One after another the six horses of their outfit appeared out of the timber, and last of all rode the mountain man. He was gathered like a partly released spring in his saddle, an attitude born of years in the mountains, and because of a certain difficulty he had in distributing gracefully his six-foot-two-inch length of flesh and bone astride a mountain cayuse.

Upon his appearance Langdon dismounted, and turned his eyes again up the valley. The stubbly blond beard on his face did not conceal the deep tan painted there by weeks of exposure in the mountains; he had opened his shirt at the throat, exposing a neck darkened by sun and wind; his eyes were of a keen, searching blue-gray, and they quested the country ahead of him now with the joyous intentness of the hunter and the adventurer.

Langdon was thirty-five. A part of his life he spent in the wild places; the other part he spent in writing about the things he found there. His companion was five years his junior in age, but had the better of him by six inches in length of anatomy, if those additional inches could be called an advantage. Bruce thought they were not. "The devil of it is I ain't done growin' yet!" he often explained.

He rode up now and unlimbered himself. Langdon pointed ahead.

"Did you ever see anything to beat that?" he asked.

"Fine country," agreed Bruce. "Mighty good place to camp, too, Jim. There ought to be caribou in this range, an' bear. We need some fresh meat. Gimme a match, will you?"

It had come to be a habit with them to light both their pipes with one match when possible. They performed this ceremony now while viewing the situation. As he puffed the first luxurious cloud of smoke from his bulldog, Langdon nodded toward the timber from which they had just come.

"Fine place for our tepee," he said. "Dry wood, running water, and the first good balsam we've struck in a week for our beds. We can hobble the horses in that little open plain we crossed a quarter of a mile back. I saw plenty of buffalo grass and a lot of wild timothy."

He looked at his watch.

"It's only three o'clock. We might go on. But—what do you say? Shall we stick for a day or two, and see what this country looks like?"

"Looks good to me," said Bruce.

He sat down as he spoke, with his back to a rock, and over his knee he leveled a long brass telescope. From his saddle Langdon unslung a binocular glass imported from Paris. The telescope was a relic of the Civil War. Together, their shoulders touching as they steadied themselves against the rock, they studied the rolling slopes and the green slides of the mountains ahead of them.

They were in Big Game country, and what Langdon called the Unknown. So far as he and Bruce Otto could discover, no other white man had ever preceded them. It was a country shut in by tremendous ranges,

15

through which it had taken them twenty days of sweating toil to make a hundred miles.

That afternoon they had crossed the summit of the Great Divide that split the skies north and south, and through their glasses they were looking now upon the first green slopes and wonderful peaks of the Firepan Mountains. To the northward—and they had been traveling north—was the Skeena River; on the west and south were the Babine range and waterways; eastward, over the Divide, was the Driftwood, and still farther eastward the Ominica range and the tributaries of the Finley. They had started from civilization on the tenth day of May and this was the thirtieth of June.

As Langdon looked through his glasses he believed that at last they had reached the bourne of their desires. For nearly two months they had worked to get beyond the trails of men, and they had succeeded. There were no hunters here. There were no prospectors. The valley ahead of them was filled with golden promise, and as he sought out the first of its mystery and its wonder his heart was filled with the deep and satisfying joy which only men like Langdon can fully understand. To his friend and comrade, Bruce Otto, with whom he had gone five times into the North country, all mountains and all valleys were very much alike; he was born among them, he had lived among them all his life, and he would probably die among them.

It was Bruce who gave him a sudden sharp nudge with his elbow.

"I see the heads of three caribou crossing a dip

about a mile and a half up the valley," he said, without taking his eyes from the telescope.

"And I see a nanny and her kid on the black shale of that first mountain to the right," replied Langdon. "And, by George, there's a sky pilot looking down on her from a crag a thousand feet above the shale! He's got a beard a foot long. Bruce, I'll bet we've struck a regular Garden of Eden!"

"Looks it," vouchsafed Bruce, coiling up his long legs to get a better rest for his telescope. "If this ain't a sheep an' bear country, I've made the worst guess I ever made in my life."

For five minutes they looked, without a word passing between them. Behind them their horses were nibbling hungrily in the thick, rich grass. The sound of the many waters in the mountains droned in their ears, and the valley seemed sleeping in a sea of sunshine. Langdon could think of nothing more comparable than that—slumber. The valley was like a great, comfortable, happy cat, and the sounds they heard, all commingling in that pleasing drone, were its drowsy purring. He was focusing his glass a little more closely on the goat standing watchfully on its crag, when Otto spoke again.

"I see a grizzly as big as a house!" he announced quietly.

Bruce seldom allowed his equanimity to be disturbed, except by the packhorses. Thrilling news like this he always introduced as unconcernedly as though speaking of a bunch of violets.

Langdon sat up with a jerk.

"Where?" he demanded.

He leaned over to get the range of the other's telescope, every nerve in his body suddenly aquiver.

"See that slope on the second shoulder, just beyond the ravine over there?" said Bruce, with one eye closed and the other still glued to the telescope.

"He's halfway up, digging out a gopher."

Langdon focused his glass on the slope, and a moment later an excited gasp came from him.

"See 'im?" asked Bruce.

"The glass has pulled him within four feet of my nose," replied Langdon. "Bruce, that's the biggest grizzly in the Rocky Mountains!"

"If he ain't, he's his twin brother," chuckled the packer, without moving a muscle. "He beats your eight-footer by a dozen inches, Jimmy! An'"—he paused at this psychological moment to pull a plug of black MacDonald from his pocket and bite off a mouthful, without taking his telescope from his eye— "an' the wind is in our favor an' he's as busy as a flea!" he finished.

Otto unwound himself and rose to his feet, and Langdon jumped up briskly. In such situations as this there was a mutual understanding between them which made words unnecessary. They led the eight horses back into the edge of the timber and tied them there, took their rifles from the leather holsters, and each was careful to put a sixth cartridge in the chamber of his weapon. Then for a matter of two minutes they both studied the slope and its approaches with their naked eyes.

"We can slip up the ravine," suggested Langdon.

Bruce nodded.

"I reckon it's a three-hundred-yard shot from there," he said. "It's the best we can do. He'd get our wind if we went below 'im. If it was a couple o' hours earlier—"

"We'd climb over the mountain and come down on him from *above*!" exclaimed Langdon, laughing. "Bruce, you're the most senseless idiot on the face of the globe when it comes to climbing mountains! You'd climb over Hardesty or Geikie to shoot a goat from *above*, even though you could get him from the valley without any work at all. I'm glad it isn't morning. We can get that bear from the ravine!"

"Mebbe," said Bruce, and they started.

They walked openly over the green, flower-carpeted meadows ahead of them. The wind had shifted, and was almost in their faces. Their swift walk changed to a dogtrot, and they swung in nearer to the slope, so that for fifteen minutes a huge knoll concealed the grizzly. In another ten minutes they came to the ravine, a narrow, rock-littered and precipitous gully worn in the mountainside by centuries of spring floods gushing down from the snow-peaks above. Here they made cautious observations.

The big grizzly was perhaps six hundred yards up the slope, and pretty close to three hundred yards from the nearest point reached by the gully.

Bruce spoke in a whisper now.

"You go up an' do the stalkin', Jimmy," he said. "That bear's goin' to do one of two things if you miss or only wound 'im—one o' three, mebbe: he's going to investigate *you*, or he's going up over the break, or he's comin' down in the valley—this way. We can't keep 'im from goin' over the break, an' if he tackles you—just summerset it down the gully. You can beat 'im out. He's most apt to come this way if you don't get 'im, so I'll wait here. Good luck to you, Jimmy!"

With this he went out and crouched behind a rock, where he could keep an eye on the grizzly, and Langdon began to climb quietly up the boulder-strewn gully.

CHAPTER
THREE

OF ALL the living creatures in this sleeping valley, Thor was the busiest. He was a bear with individuality, you might say. Like some people, he went to bed very early; he began to get sleepy in October, and turned in for his long nap in November. He slept until April, and usually was a week or ten days behind other bears in waking. He was a sound sleeper, and when awake he was very wide awake. During April and May he permitted himself to doze considerably in the warmth of sunny rocks, but from the beginning of June until the middle of September he closed his eyes in real sleep just about four hours out of every twelve.

He was very busy as Langdon began his cautious climb up the gully. He had succeeded in getting his gopher, a fat, aldermanic old patriarch who had disappeared in one crunch and a gulp, and he was now absorbed in finishing off his day's feast with an occasional fat, white grub and a few sour ants captured from under stones which he turned over with his paw.

In his search after these delicacies Thor used his right paw in turning over the rocks. Ninety-nine out of every hundred bears—probably a hundred and ninety-nine out of every two hundred—are left-handed; Thor was right-handed. This gave him an advantage in fighting, in fishing, and in stalking meat, for a grizzly's right arm is longer than his left—so much longer that if he lost his sixth sense of orientation he would be constantly traveling in a circle.

In his quest Thor was headed for the gully. His huge head hung close to the ground. At short distances his vision was microscopic in its keenness; his olfactory nerves were so sensitive that he could catch one of the big rock-ants with his eyes shut.

He would choose the flat rocks mostly. His huge right paw, with its long claws, was as clever as a human hand. The stone lifted, a sniff or two, a lick of his hot, flat tongue, and he ambled on to the next.

He took this work with tremendous seriousness, much like an elephant hunting for peanuts hidden in a bale of hay. He saw no humor in the operation. As a matter of fact, Nature had not intended there should be any humor about it. Thor's time was more or less valueless, and during the course of a summer he absorbed in his system a good many hundred thousand sour ants, sweet grubs, and juicy insects of various kinds, not to mention a host of gophers and still tinier rock-rabbits. These small things all added to the huge rolls of fat which it was necessary for him to store up for that "absorptive consumption" which kept him alive during his long winter sleep. This was why Nature had made his little greenish-brown eyes twin microscopes, infallible at distances of a few feet, and almost worthless at a thousand yards.

As he was about to turn a fresh stone Thor paused in his operations. For a full minute he stood nearly motionless. Then his head swung slowly, his nose close to the ground. Very faintly he had caught an exceedingly pleasing odor. It was so faint that he was afraid of losing it if he moved. So he stood until he was sure of himself, then he swung his huge shoulders around and descended two yards down the slope, swinging his head slowly from right to left, and sniffing. The scent grew stronger. Another two yards down the slope he found it very strong under a rock. It was a big rock, and weighed probably two hundred pounds. Thor dragged it aside with his one right hand as if it were no more than a pebble.

Instantly there was a wild and protesting chatter, and a tiny striped rock-rabbit, very much like a chipmunk, darted away just as Thor's left hand came down with a smash that would have broken the neck of a caribou.

It was not the scent of the rock-rabbit, but the savor of what the rock-rabbit had stored under the stone that had attracted Thor. And this booty still remained—a half-pint of ground-nuts piled carefully in a little hollow lined with moss. They were not really nuts. They were more like diminutive potatoes, about the size of cherries, and very much like potatoes in appearance. They were starchy and sweet, and fattening. Thor enjoyed them immensely, rumbling in that curious satisfied way deep down in his chest as he feasted. And then he resumed his quest.

He did not hear Langdon as the hunter came nearer and nearer up the broken gully. He did not smell him, for the wind was fatally wrong. He had forgotten the noxious man-smell that had disturbed and irritated him an hour before. He was quite happy; he was good-humored; he was fat and sleek. An irritable, cross-grained, and quarrelsome bear is always thin. The true hunter knows him as soon as he sets eyes on him. He is like the rogue elephant.

Thor continued his food-seeking, edging still closer to the gully. He was within a hundred and fifty yards of it when a sound suddenly brought him alert. Langdon, in his effort to creep up the steep side of the gully for a shot, had accidentally loosened a rock. It went crashing down the ravine, starting other stones that followed in a noisy clatter. At the foot of the coulee, six hundred yards down, Bruce swore softly under his breath. He saw Thor sit up. At that distance he was going to shoot if the bear made for the break.

For thirty seconds Thor sat on his haunches. Then he started for the ravine, ambling slowly and deliberately. Langdon, panting and inwardly cursing at his ill luck, struggled to make the last ten feet to the edge of the slope. He heard Bruce yell, but he could not make out the warning. Hands and feet he dug fiercely into shale and rock as he fought to make those last three or four yards as quickly as possible.

He was almost to the top when he paused for a moment and turned his eyes upward. His heart went into his throat, and he started. For ten seconds he could not move. Directly over him was a monster head and a huge hulk of shoulder. Thor was looking down on him, his jaws agape, his finger-long fangs snarling, his eyes burning with a greenish-red fire.

In that moment Thor saw his first of man. His great lungs were filled with the hot smell of him, and suddenly he turned away from that smell as if from a plague. With his rifle half under him Langdon had had no opportunity to shoot. Wildly he clambered up the remaining few feet. The shale and stones slipped and slid under him. It was a matter of sixty seconds before he pulled himself over the top.

Thor was a hundred yards away, speeding in a rolling, ball-like motion toward the break. From the foot of the coulee came the sharp crack of Otto's rifle. Langdon squatted quickly, raising his left knee for a rest, and at a hundred and fifty yards began firing.

Sometimes it happens that an hour—a minute—changes the destiny of man; and the ten seconds which followed swiftly after the first shot from the foot of the coulee changed Thor. He had got his fill of the man-smell. He had seen man. And now he *felt* him.

It was as if one of the lightning flashes he had often seen splitting the dark skies had descended upon him and had entered his flesh like a red-hot knife; and with that first burning agony of pain came the strange, echoing roar of the rifles. He had turned up the slope when the bullet had struck him in the fore-shoulder, mushrooming its deadly soft point against his tough hide, and tearing a hole through his flesh—but without touching the bone. He was two hundred yards from the ravine when it hit; he was nearer three hundred when the stinging fire seared him again, this time in his flank.

Neither shot had staggered his huge bulk; twenty such shots would not have killed him. But the second stopped him, and he turned with a roar of rage that was like the bellowing of a mad bull—a snarling, thunderous cry of wrath that could have been heard a quarter of a mile down the valley.

Bruce heard it as he fired his sixth unavailing shot at seven hundred yards. Langdon was reloading. For fifteen seconds Thor offered himself openly, roaring his defiance, challenging the enemy he could no longer see; and then at Langdon's seventh shot, a whiplash of fire raked his back, and in strange dread of this lightning which he could not fight, Thor continued up over the break. He heard other rifle shots, which were like a new kind of thunder. But he was not hit again. Painfully he began the descent into the next valley.

Thor knew that he was hurt, but he could not comprehend that hurt. Once in the descent he paused for a few moments, and a pool of blood dripped upon the ground under his foreleg. He sniffed at it suspiciously and wonderingly.

He swung eastward, and a little later he caught a fresh taint of the man-smell in the air. The wind was bringing it to him now, and in spite of the fact that he wanted to lie down and nurse his wound he ambled on a little faster, for he had learned one thing that he would never forget: the man-smell and his hurt had come together.

He reached the bottoms, and buried himself in the

thick timber; and then, crossing the timber, he came to a creek. Perhaps a hundred times he had traveled up and down this creek. It was the main trail that led from one half of his range to the other.

Instinctively he always took this trail when he was hurt or when he was sick, and also when he was ready to den up for the winter. There was one chief reason for this: he was born in the almost impenetrable fastnesses at the head of the creek, and his cubhood had been spent amid its brambles of wild currants and soap berries and its rich red ground carpets of kinnikinic. It was home. In it he was alone. It was the one part of his domain that he held inviolate from all other bears. He tolerated other bears—blacks and grizzlies—on the wider and sunnier slopes of his range just so long as they moved on when he approached. They might seek food there, and nap in the sun-pools, and live in quiet and peace if they did not defy his suzerainty.

Thor did not drive other bears from his range, except when it was necessary to demonstrate again that he was High Mogul. This happened occasionally, and there was a fight. And always after a fight Thor came into this valley and went up the creek to cure his wounds.

He made his way more slowly than usual today. There was a terrible pain in his fore-shoulder. Now and then it hurt him so that his leg doubled up, and he stumbled. Several times he waded shoulder-deep into pools and let the cold water run over his wounds. Gradually they stopped bleeding. But the pain grew worse.

Thor's best friend in such an emergency was a clay wallow. This was the second reason why he always took this trail when he was sick or hurt. It led to the clay wallow. And the clay wallow was his doctor.

The sun was setting before he reached the wallow. His jaws hung open a little. His great head drooped lower. He had lost a great deal of blood. He was tired, and his shoulder hurt him so badly that he wanted to tear with his teeth at the strange fire that was consuming it.

The clay wallow was twenty or thirty feet in diameter, and hollowed into a little shallow pool in the center. It was a soft, cool, golden-colored clay, and Thor waded into it to his armpits. Then he rolled over gently on his wounded side. The clay touched his hurt like a cooling salve. It sealed the cut, and Thor gave a great heaving gasp of relief. For a long time he lay in that soft bed of clay. The sun went down, darkness came, and the wonderful stars filled the sky. And still Thor lay there, nursing that first hurt of man.

CHAPTER
FOUR

IN THE edge of the balsam and spruce Langdon and Otto sat smoking their pipes after supper, with the glowing embers of a fire at their feet. The night air in these higher altitudes of the mountains had grown chilly, and Bruce rose long enough to throw a fresh armful of dry spruce on the coals. Then he stretched out his long form again, with his head and shoulders bolstered comfortably against the butt of a tree, and for the fiftieth time he chuckled.

"Chuckle an' be blasted," growled Langdon. "I tell you I hit him twice, Bruce—twice anyway; and I was at a devilish disadvantage!"

" 'Specially when 'e was lookin' down an' grinnin' in your face," retorted Bruce, who had enjoyed hugely his comrade's ill luck. "Jimmy, at that distance you should a'most ha' killed 'im with a rock!"

"My gun was under me," explained Langdon for the twentieth time.

"W'ich ain't just the proper place for a gun to be when yo'r hunting a grizzly," reminded Bruce.

"The gully was confoundedly steep. I had to dig in

with both feet and my fingers. If it had been any steeper I would have used my teeth."

Langdon sat up, knocked the ash out of the bowl of his pipe, and reloaded it with fresh tobacco.

"Bruce, that's the biggest grizzly in the Rocky Mountains!"

"He'd 'a' made a fine rug in your den, Jimmy—if yo'r gun hadn't 'appened to 'ave been under you."

"And I'm going to have him in my den before I finish," declared Langdon. "I've made up my mind. We'll make a permanent camp here. I'm going to get that grizzly if it takes all summer. I'd rather have him than any other ten bears in the Firepan Range. He was a nine-footer if an inch. His head was as big as a a bushel basket, and the hair on his shoulders was four inches long. I don't know that I'm sorry I didn't kill him. He's hit, and he'll surely fight shy. There'll be a lot of fun in getting him."

"There will that," agreed Bruce, " 'specially if you meet 'im again during the next week or so, while he's still sore from the bullets. Better not have the gun under you then, Jimmy!"

"What do you say to making this a permanent camp?"

"Couldn't be better. Plenty of fresh meat, good grazing, and fine water." After a moment he added: "He was hit pretty hard. He was bleedin' bad at the summit."

In the firelight Langdon began cleaning his rifle.

"You think he may clear out—leave the country?"

Bruce emitted a grunt of disgust.

"Clear out? *Run away?* Mebbe he would if he was a

black. But he's a grizzly, and the boss of this country. He may fight shy of this valley for a while, but you can bet he ain't goin' to emigrate. The harder you hit a grizzly the madder he gets, an' if you keep on hittin' 'im he keeps on gettin' madder, until he drops dead. If you want that bear bad enough we can surely get him."

"I do," Langdon reiterated with emphasis. "He'll smash record measurements or I miss my guess. I want him, and I want him bad, Bruce. Do you think we'll be able to trail him in the morning?"

Bruce shook his head.

"It won't be a matter of trailing," he said. "It's just simply *hunt*. After a grizzly has been hit he keeps movin'. He won't go out of his range, an' neither is he going to show himself on the open slopes like that up there. Metoosin ought to be along with the dogs inside of three or four days, an' when we get that bunch of Airedales in action, there'll be some fun."

Langdon sighted at the fire through the polished barrel of his rifle, and said doubtfully:

"I've been having my doubts about Metoosin for a week back. We've come through some mighty rough country."

"That old Indian could follow our trail if we traveled on rock," declared Bruce confidently. "He'll be here inside o' three days, barring the dogs don't run their fool heads into too many porcupines. An' when they come"—he rose and stretched his gaunt frame— "we'll have the biggest time we ever had in our lives. I'm just guessin' these mount'ins are so full o' bear that them ten dogs will all be massacreed within a week. Want to bet?"

Langdon closed his rifle with a snap.

"I only want one bear," he said, ignoring the challenge, "and I have an idea we'll get him tomorrow. You're the bear specialist of the outfit, Bruce, but I think he was too hard hit to travel far."

They had made two beds of soft balsam boughs near the fire, and Langdon now followed his companion's example, and began spreading his blankets. It had been a hard day, and within five minutes after stretching himself out he was alseep.

He was still asleep when Bruce rolled out from under his blanket at dawn. Without rousing Langdon the young packer slipped on his boots and waded back a quarter of a mile through the heavy dew to round up the horses. When he returned he brought Dishpan and their saddle-horses with him. By that time Langdon was up, and starting a fire.

Langdon frequently reminded himself that such mornings as this had made him disappoint the doctors and rob the grave. Just eight years ago this June he had come into the North for the first time, thin-chested and with a bad lung. "You can go if you insist, young man," one of the doctors had told him, "but you're going to your own funeral." And now he had a five-inch expansion and was as tough as a knot. The first rose tints of the sun were creeping over the mountaintops; the air was filled with the sweetness of flowers, and dew, and growing things, and his lungs drew in deep breaths of oxygen laden with the tonic and perfume of balsam.

He was more demonstrative than his companion in the joyousness of this wild life. It made him want to shout, and sing, and whistle. He restrained himself this morning. The thrill of the hunt was in his blood.

While Otto saddled the horses Langdon made the bannock. He had become an expert at what he called "wild-bread" baking, and his method possessed the double efficiency of saving both waste and time.

He opened one of the heavy flour sacks, made a hollow in the flour with his two doubled fists, partly filled this hollow with a pint of water and half a cupful of caribou grease, added a tablespoonful of baking powder and a three-finger pinch of salt, and began to mix. Inside of five minutes he had the bannock loaves in the big tin reflector, and half an hour later the sheep steaks were fried, the potatoes done, and the bannock baked to a golden brown.

The sun was just showing its face in the east when they trailed out of camp. They rode across the valley, but walked up the slope, the horses following obediently in their footsteps.

It was not difficult to pick up Thor's trail. Where he had paused to snarl back defiance at his enemies there was a big red spatter on the ground; from this point to the summit they followed a crimson thread of blood. Three times in descending into the other valley they found where Thor had stopped, and each time they saw where a pool of blood had soaked into the earth or run over the rock.

They passed through the timber and came to the creek, and here, in a strip of firm black sand, Thor's footprints brought them to a pause. Bruce stared. An exclamation of amazement came from Langdon, and without a word having passed between them he drew

34

out his pocket-tape and knelt beside one of the tracks.

"Fifteen and a quarter inches!" he gasped.

"Measure another," said Bruce.

"Fifteen and—a half!"

Bruce looked up the gorge.

"The biggest I ever see was fourteen an' a half," he said, and there was a touch of awe in his voice. "He was shot up the Athabasca an' he's stood as the biggest grizzly ever killed in British Columbia. Jimmy, *this one beats 'im!*"

They went on, and measured the tracks again at the edge of the first pool where Thor had bathed his wounds. There was almost no variation in his measurements. Only occasionally after this did they find spots of blood. It was ten o'clock when they came to the clay wallow and saw where Thor had made his bed in it.

"He was pretty sick," said Bruce in a low voice. "He was here most all night."

Moved by the same impulse and the same thought, they looked ahead of them. Half a mile farther on the mountains closed in until the gorge between them was dark and sunless.

"He was pretty sick," repeated Bruce, still looking ahead. "Mebbe we'd better tie the horses an' go on alone. It's possible—he's in there."

They tied the horses to scrub cedars, and relieved Dishpan of her pack.

Then, with their rifles in readiness, and eyes and ears alert, they went on cautiously into the silence and gloom of the gorge.

CHAPTER
FIVE

THOR had gone up the gorge at daybreak. He was stiff when he rose from the clay wallow, but a good deal of the burning and pain had gone from his wound. It still hurt him, but not as it had hurt him the preceding evening. His discomfort was not all in his shoulder, and it was not in any one place in particular. He was *sick*, and had he been human he would have been in bed with a thermometer under this tongue and a doctor holding his pulse. He walked up the gorge slowly and laggingly. An indefatigable seeker of food, he no longer thought of food. He was not hungry, and he did not want to eat.

With his hot tongue he lapped frequently at the cool water of the creek, and even more frequently he turned half about and sniffed the wind. He knew that the man-smell and the strange thunder and the still more inexplicable lightning lay behind him. All night he had been on guard, and he was cautious now.

For a particular hurt Thor knew of no particular

remedy. He was not a botanist in the finer sense of the word, but in creating him the Spirit of the Wild had ordained that he should be his own physician. As a cat seeks catnip, so Thor sought certain things when he was not feeling well. All bitterness is not quinine, but certainly bitter things were Thor's remedies, and as he made his way up the gorge his nose hung close to the ground, and he sniffed in the low copses and thick bush-tangles he passed.

He came to a small green spot covered with kinnikinic, a ground plant two inches high which bore red berries as big as a small pea. They were not red now, but green; bitter as gall, and contained an astringent tonic called uvaursi. Thor ate them.

After that he found soap berries growing on bushes that looked very much like currant bushes. The fruit was already larger than currants, and turning pink. Indians ate these berries when they had fever, and Thor gathered half a pint before he went on. They, too, were bitter. He nosed the trees, and found at last what he wanted. It was a jackpine, and at several places within his reach the fresh pitch was oozing. A bear seldom passes a bleeding jackpine. It is his chief tonic, and Thor licked the fresh pitch with his tongue. In this way he absorbed not only turpentine, but also, in a roundabout sort of a way, a whole pharmacopoeia of medicines made from this particular element.

By the time he arrived at the end of the gorge Thor's stomach was a fairly well-stocked drug emporium. Among other things he had eaten perhaps half a quart of spruce and balsam needles. When a dog is sick he eats grass; when a bear is sick he eats

38

pine or balsam needles if he can get them. Also he pads his stomach and intestines with them in the last hour before denning himself away for the winter.

The sun was not yet up when Thor came to the end of the gorge, and stood for a few moments at the mouth of a low cave that reached back into the wall of the mountain. How far his memory went back it would be impossible to say; but in the whole world, as he knew it, this cave was home. It was not more than four feet high, and twice as wide, but it was many times as deep and was carpeted with a soft white floor of sand. In some past age a little stream had trickled out of this cavern, and the far end of it made a comfortable bedroom for a sleeping bear when the temperature was fifty degrees below zero.

Ten years before Thor's mother had gone in there to sleep through the winter, and when she waddled out to get her first glimpse of spring three little cubs waddled with her. Thor was one of them. He was still half blind, for it is five weeks after a grizzly cub is born before he can see; and there was not much hair on his body, for a grizzly cub is born as naked as a human baby. His eyes open and his hair begins to grow at just about the same time. Since then Thor had denned eight times in that cavern home.

He wanted to go in now. He wanted to lie down in the far end of it and wait until he felt better. For perhaps two or three minutes he hesitated, sniffing yearningly at the door to his cave, and then feeling the wind from down the gorge. Something told him that he should go on.

To the westward there was a sloping ascent up out

of the gorge to the summit, and Thor climbed this. The sun was well up when he reached the top, and for a little while he rested again and looked down on the other half of his domain.

Even more wonderful was this valley than the one into which Bruce and Langdon had ridden a few hours before. From range to range it was a good two miles in width, and in the opposite directions it stretched away in a great rolling panorama of gold and green and black. From where Thor stood it was like an immense park. Green slopes reached almost to the summits of the mountains, and to a point half-way up these slopes—the last timberline—clumps of spruce and balsam trees were scattered over the green as if set there by the hands of men. Some of these timber-patches were no larger than the decorative clumps in a city park, and others covered acres and tens of acres; and at the foot of the slopes on either side, like decorative fringes, were thin and unbroken lines of forest. Between these two lines of forest lay the open valley of soft and undulating meadow, dotted with its purplish bosks of buffalo willow and mountain sage, its green coppices of wild rose and thorn, and its clumps of trees. In the hollow of the valley ran a stream.

Thor descended about four hundred yards from where he stood, and then turned northward along the green slope, so that he was traveling from patch to patch of the parklike timber, a hundred and fifty or two hundred yards above the fringe of forest. To this height, midway between the meadows in the valley and the first shale and bare rock of the peaks, he came most frequently on his small game hunts.

Like fat woodchucks the whistlers were already beginning to sun themselves on their rocks. Their long, soft, elusive whistlings, pleasant to hear above the drone of mountain waters, filled the air with a musical cadence. Now and then one would whistle shrilly and warningly close at hand, and then flatten himself out on his rock as the big bear passed, and for a few moments no whistling would break upon the gentle purring of the valley.

But Thor was giving no thought to the hunt this morning. Twice he encountered porcupines, the sweetest of all morsels to him, and passed them unnoticed; the warm, *sleeping* smell of a caribou came hot and fresh from a thicket, but he did not approach the thicket to investigate; out of a coulee, narrow and dark, like a black ditch, he caught the scent of a badger. For two hours he traveled steadily northward along the half-crest of the slopes before he struck down through the timber to the stream.

The clay adhering to his wound was beginning to harden, and again he waded shoulder-deep into a pool, and stood there for several minutes. The water washed most of the clay away. For another two hours he followed the creek, drinking frequently. Then came the *sapoos oowin*—six hours after he had left the clay wallow. The kinnikinic berries, the soap berries, the jackpine pitch, the spruce and balsam needles, and the water he had drunk, all mixed in his stomach in one big compelling dose, brought it about—and Thor felt tremendously better, so much better that for the first time he turned and growled back in the direction of his enemies. His shoulder still hurt him, but his sickness was gone.

For many minutes after the *sapoos oowin* he stood without moving, and many times he growled. The snarling rumble deep in his chest had a new meaning now. Until last night and today he had not known a real hatred. He had fought other bears, but the fighting was not hate. It came quickly, and passed away quickly; it left no growing ugliness; he licked the wounds of a clawed enemy, and was quite frequently happy while he nursed them. But this new thing that was born in him was different.

With an unforgettable and ferocious hatred he hated the thing that had hurt him. He hated the man-smell; he hated the strange, white-faced thing he had seen clinging to the side of the gorge; and his hatred included everything associated with them. It was a hatred born of instinct and roused sharply from its long slumber by experience.

Without ever having seen or smelled man before, he knew that man was his deadliest enemy, and to be feared more than all the wild things in the mountains. He would fight the biggest grizzly. He would turn on the fiercest pack of wolves. He would brave flood and fire without flinching. But before man he must flee! He must hide! He must constantly guard himself in the peaks and on the plains with eyes and ears and nose!

Why he sensed this, why he understood all at once that a creature had come into his world, a pigmy in size, yet more to be dreaded than any foe he had ever known, was a miracle which nature alone could explain. It was a hearkening back in the age-dimmed mental fabric of Thor's race to the earliest days of man—man, first of all, with the club; man with the spear hardened in fire; man with the flint-tipped arrow; man with the trap and the deadfall, and, lastly, man with the gun. Through all the ages man had been his one and only master. Nature had impressed it upon him—had been impressing it upon him through a hundred or a thousand or ten thousand generations.

And now for the first time in his life that dormant part of his instinct leaped into warning wakefulness, and he understood. He hated man, and hereafter he would hate everything that bore the man-smell. And with this hate there was also born in him for the first time *fear*. Had man never pushed Thor and his kind to the death the world would not have known him as Ursus Horribilis the Terrible.

Thor still followed the creek, nosing along slowly and lumberingly, but very steadily; his head and neck bent low, his huge rear quarters rising and falling in that rolling motion peculiar to all bears, and especially so of the grizzly. His long claws click-click-clicked on the stones; he crunched heavily in the gravel; in soft sand he left enormous footprints.

That part of the valley which he was now entering held a particular significance for Thor, and he began to loiter, pausing often to sniff the air on all sides of him. He was not a monogamist, but for many mating seasons past he had come to find his *Iskwao* in this wonderful sweep of meadow and plain between the two ranges. He could always expect her in July, waiting for him or seeking him with that strange savage longing of motherhood in her breast. She was a splendid grizzly who came from the western ranges when the spirit of mating days called; big, and strong, and of a beautiful golden-brown color, so that the children of Thor and his *Iskwao* were the finest young grizzlies in all the mountains. The mother took them back with her unborn, and they opened their eyes and lived and fought in the valleys and on the slopes far to the west. If in later years Thor ever chased his own children out of his hunting grounds, or whipped them in a fight, Nature kindly blinded him to the fact. He was like most grouchy old bachelors: he did not like small folk. He tolerated a little cub as a cross-grained old woman-hater might have tolerated a pink baby; but he wasn't as cruel as Punch, for he had never killed a cub. He had cuffed them soundly whenever they had dared to come within reach of him, but always with the flat, soft palm of his paw, and with just enough force behind it to send them keeling over and over like little round fluffy balls.

This was Thor's only expression of displeasure when a strange mother-bear invaded his range with her cubs. In other ways he was quite chivalrous. He would not drive the mother-bear and her cubs away, and he would not fight with her, no matter how shrewish or unpleasant she was. Even if he found them eating at one of his kills, he would do nothing more than give the cubs a sound cuffing.

All this is somewhat necessary to show with what

sudden and violent agitation Thor caught a certain warm, close smell as he came around the end of a mass of huge boulders. He stopped, turned his head, and swore in his low, growling way. Six feet from him, groveling flat in a patch of white sand, wriggling and shaking for all the world like a half-frightened puppy that had not yet made up its mind whether it had met a friend or an enemy, was a lone bear cub. It was not more than three months old—altogether too young to be away from its mother; and it had a sharp little tan face and a white spot on its baby breast which marked it as a member of the black bear family, and not a grizzly.

The cub was trying as hard as it could to say, "I am lost, strayed, or stolen; I'm hungry, and I've got a porcupine quill in my foot," but in spite of that, with another ominous growl, Thor began to look about the rocks for the mother. She was not in sight, and neither could he smell her, two facts that turned his great head again toward the cub.

Muskwa—an Indian would have called the cub that—had crawled a foot or two nearer on his little belly. He greeted Thor's second inspection with a genial wriggling which carried him forward another half foot, and a low warning rumbled in Thor's chest. "Don't come any nearer," it said plainly enough, "or I'll keel you over!"

Muskwa understood. He lay as if dead, his nose and paws and belly flat on the sand, and Thor looked about him again. When his eyes returned to Muskwa, the cub was within three feet of him, squirming flat in the sand and whimpering softly. Thor lifted his right paw four inches from the ground. "Another inch and I'll give you a welt!" he growled.

Muskwa wriggled and trembled; he licked his lips with his tiny red tongue, half in fear and half pleading for mercy, and in spite of Thor's lifted paw he wormed his way another six inches nearer.

There was a sort of rattle instead of a growl in Thor's throat. His heavy hand fell to the sand. A third time he looked about and sniffed the air; he growled again. Any crusty old bachelor would have understood that growl. "Now where the devil is the kid's mother!" it said.

Something happened then. Muskwa had crept close to Thor's wounded leg. He rose up, and his nose caught the scent of the raw wound. Gently his tongue touched it. It was like velvet—that tongue. It was wonderfully pleasant to feel, and Thor stood there for many moments, making neither movement nor sound while the cub licked his wound. Then he lowered his great hand. He sniffed the little ball of friendship that had come to him. Muskwa whined in a motherless way. Thor growled, but more softly now. It was no longer a threat. The heat of his great tongue fell once on the cub's face.

"Come on!" he said, and resumed his journey into the north.

And close at his heels followed the motherless little tan-faced cub.

CHAPTER
SIX

THE creek which Thor was following was a tributary of the Babine, and he was headed pretty nearly straight for the Skeena. As he was traveling upstream the country was becoming higher and rougher. He had come perhaps seven or eight miles from the summit of the divide when he found Muskwa. From this point the slopes began to assume a different aspect. They were cut up by dark, narrow gullies, and broken by enormous masses of rocks, jagged cliffs, and steep slides of shale. The creek became noisier and more difficult to follow.

Thor was now entering one of his strongholds: a region which contained a thousand hiding-places, if he had wanted to hide; a wild, uptorn country where it was not difficult for him to kill big game, and where he was certain that the man-smell would not follow him.

For half an hour after leaving the mass of rocks where he had encountered Muskwa, Thor lumbered on as if utterly oblivious of the fact that the cub was following. But he could hear him and smell him.

Muskwa was having a hard time of it. His fat little body and his fat little legs were unaccustomed to this sort of journeying, but he was a game youngster, and only twice did he whimper in that half-hour—once he toppled off a rock into the edge of the creek, and again when he came down too hard on the porcupine quill in his foot.

At last Thor abandoned the creek and turned up a deep ravine, which he followed until he came to a dip, or plateaulike plain, halfway up a broad slope. Here he found a rock on the sunny side of a grassy knoll, and stopped. It may be that little Muskwa's babyish friendship, the caress of his soft little red tongue at just the psychological moment, and his perseverance in following Thor had all combined to touch a responsive chord in the other's big brute heart, for after nosing about restlessly for a few moments Thor stretched himself out beside the rock. Not until then did the utterly exhausted little tan-faced cub lie down, but when he did lie down he was so dead tired that he was sound asleep in three minutes.

Twice again during the early part of the afternoon the *sapoos oowin* worked on Thor, and he began to feel hungry. It was not the sort of hunger to be appeased by ants and grubs, or even gophers and whistlers. It may be, too, that he guessed how nearly starved little Muskwa was. The cub had not once opened his eyes, and he still lay in his warm pool of sunshine when Thor made up his mind to go on.

It was about three o'clock, a particularly quiet and drowsy part of a late June or early July day in a northern mountain valley. The whistlers had piped until they were tired, and lay squat out in the sunshine on their rocks; the eagles soared so high above the peaks that they were mere dots; the hawks, with meat-filled crops, had disappeared into the timber; goat and sheep were lying down far up toward the skyline, and if there were any grazing animals near they were well fed and napping.

The mountain hunter knew that this was the hour when he should scan the green slopes and the open places between the clumps of timber for bears, and especially for flesh-eating bears.

It was Thor's chief prospecting hour. Instinct told him that when all other creatures were well fed and napping he could move more openly and with less fear of detection. He could find his game, and watch it. Occasionally he would kill a goat or a sheep or a caribou in broad daylight, for over short distances he could run faster than either a goat or a sheep, and as fast as a caribou. But chiefly he killed at sunset or in the darkness of early evening.

Thor rose from beside the rock with a prodigious whoof that roused Muskwa. The cub got up, blinked at Thor and then at the sun, and shook himself until he fell down.

Thor eyed the black and tan mite a bit sourly. After the *sapoos oowin* he was craving red, juicy flesh, just as a very hungry man yearns for a thick porterhouse instead of lady fingers or mayonnaise salad—flesh

49

and plenty of it; and how he could hunt down and kill a caribou with that half-starved but very much interested cub at his heels puzzled him.

Muskwa himself seemed to understand and answer the question. He ran a dozen yards ahead of Thor, then stopped and looked back impudently, his little ears perked forward, and with the look in his face of a small boy proving to his father that he is perfectly qualified to go on his first rabbit hunt.

With another whoof Thor started along the slope in a spurt that brought him up to Muskwa immediately, and with a sudden sweep of his right paw he sent the cub rolling a dozen feet behind him, a manner of speech that said plainly enough, "That's where you belong if you're going hunting with me!"

Then Thor lumbered slowly on, eyes and ears and nostrils keyed for the hunt. He descended until he was not more than a hundred yards above the creek, and he no longer sought out the easiest trail, but the rough and broken places. He traveled slowly and in a zigzag fashion, stealing cautiously around great masses of boulders, sniffing up each coulee that he came to, and investigating the timber clumps and windfalls.

At one time he would be so high up that he was close to the bare shale, and again so low down that he walked in the sand and gravel of the creek. He caught many scents in the wind, but none that held or deeply interested him. Once, up near the shale, he smelled goat; but he never went above the shale for meat. Twice he smelled sheep, and late in the afternoon he saw a big ram looking down on him from a precipitous crag a hundred feet above.

Lower down his nose touched the trails of porcupines, and often his head hung over the footprints of caribou as he sniffed the air ahead.

There were other bears in the valley, too. Mostly these had traveled along the creek-bottom, showing they were blacks or cinnamons. Once Thor struck the scent of another grizzly, and he rumbled ill-humoredly.

Not once in the two hours after they left the sun-rock did Thor pay any apparent attention to Muskwa, who was growing hungrier and weaker as the day lengthened. No boy that ever lived was gamer than the little tan-faced cub. In the rough places he stumbled and fell frequently; up places that Thor could make in a single step he had to fight desperately to make his way; three times Thor waded through the creek and Muskwa half drowned himself in following; he was battered and bruised and wet and his foot hurt him—but he followed. Sometimes he was close to Thor, and at others he had to run to catch up. The sun was setting when Thor at last found game, and Muskwa was almost dead.

He did not know why Thor flattened his huge bulk suddenly alongside a rock at the edge of a rough meadow, from which they could look down into a small hollow. He wanted to whimper, but he was afraid. And if he had ever wanted his mother at any time in his short life he wanted her now. He could not understand why she had left him among the rocks and had never come back; that tragedy Langdon and Bruce were to discover a little later. And he could not understand why she did not come to him now. This was just about his nursing hour before going to sleep for the night, for he was a March cub, and, according to the most approved mother-bear regulations, should have had milk for another month.

He was what Metoosin, the Indian, would have called *munookow*—that is, he was very soft. Being a bear, his birth had not been like that of other animals. His mother, like all mother-bears in a cold country, had brought him into life a long time before she had finished her winter nap in her den. He had come while she was asleep. For a month or six weeks after that, while he was still blind and naked, she had given him milk, while she herself neither ate nor drank nor saw the light of day. At the end of those six weeks she had gone forth with him from her den to seek the first mouthful of sustenance for herself. Not more than another six weeks had passed since then, and Muskwa weighed about twenty pounds—that is, he had weighed twenty pounds, but he was emptier now than he had ever been in his life, and probably weighed a little less.

Three hundred yards below Thor was a clump of balsams, a small thick patch that grew close to the edge of the miniature lake whose water crept around the farther end of the hollow. In that clump there was a caribou—perhaps two or three. Thor knew that as surely as though he saw them. The *wenipow*, or "lying down," smell of hoofed game was as different from the *nechisoo*, or "grazing smell," to Thor as day from night. One hung elusively in the air, like the faint and shifting breath of a passing woman's scented dress and hair; the other came hot and heavy, close to the earth, like the odor of a broken bottle of perfume.

Even Muskwa now caught the scent as he crept up close behind the big grizzly and lay down.

For fully ten minutes Thor did not move. His eyes took in the hollow, the edge of the lake, and the approach to the timber, and his nose gauged the wind as accurately as the pointing of a compass. The reason he remained quiet was that he was almost on the dangerline. In other words, the mountains and the sudden dip had formed a "split wind" in the hollow, and had Thor appeared fifty yards above where he now crouched, the keen-scented caribou would have got full wind of him.

With his little ears cocked forward and a new gleam of understanding in his eyes, Muskwa now looked upon his first lesson in game-stalking. Crouched so low that he seemed to be traveling on his belly, Thor moved slowly and noiselessly toward the creek, the huge ruff just forward of his shoulders standing out like the stiffened spine of a dog's back. Muskwa followed. For fully a hundred yards Thor continued his detour, and three times in that hundred yards he paused to sniff in the direction of the timber. At last he was satisfied. The wind was full in his face, and it was rich with promise.

He began to advance, in a slinking, rolling, rock-shouldered motion, taking shorter steps now, and with every muscle in his great body ready for action.

Within two minutes he reached the edge of the balsams, and there he paused again. The crackling of underbrush came distinctly. The caribou were up, but they were not alarmed. They were going forth to drink and graze.

Thor moved again, parallel to the sound. This brought him quickly to the edge of the timber, and there he stood, concealed by foliage, but with the lake and the short stretch of meadow in view. A big bull caribou came out first. His horns were half grown, and in velvet. A two-year-old followed, round and sleek and glistening like brown velvet in the sunset. For two minutes the bull stood alert, eyes, ears, and nostrils seeking for danger signals; at his heels the younger animal nibbled less suspiciously at the grass. Then lowering his head until his antlers swept back over his shoulders the old bull started slowly toward the lake for his evening drink. The two-year-old followed—and Thor came out softly from his hiding-place.

For a single moment he seemed to gather himself— and then he started. Fifty feet separated him from the caribou. He had covered half that distance like a huge rolling ball when the animals heard him. They were off like arrows sprung from the bow. But they were too late. It would have taken a swift horse to beat Thor and he had already gained momentum.

Like the wind he bore down on the flank of the two-year-old, swung a little to one side, and then without any apparent effort—still like a huge ball—he bounded in and upward, and the short race was done.

His huge right arm swung over the two-year-old's

shoulder, and as they went down his left paw gripped the caribou's muzzle like a huge human hand. Thor fell under, as he always planned to fall. He did not hug his victim to death. Just once he doubled up one of his hind legs, and when it went back the five knives it carried disemboweled the caribou. They not only disemboweled him, but twisted and broke his ribs as though they were of wood. Then Thor got up, looked around, and shook himself with a rumbling growl which might have been either a growl of triumph or an invitation for Muskwa to come to the feast.

If it was an invitation, the little tan-faced cub did not wait for a second. For the first time he smelled and tasted the warm blood of meat. And this smell and taste had come at the psychological moment in his life, just as it had come in Thor's life years before. All grizzlies are not killers of big game. In fact, very few of them are. Most of them are chiefly vegetarians, with a meat diet of smaller animals, such as gophers, whistling marmots, and porcupines. Now and then chance makes of a grizzly a hunter of caribou, goat, sheep, deer, and even moose. Such was Thor. And such, in days to come, would Muskwa be, even though he was a black and not of the family Ursus Horribilis Ord.

For an hour the two feasted, not in the ravenous way of hungry dogs, but in the slow and satisfying manner of gourmets. Muskwa, flat on his little paunch, and almost between Thor's huge forearms, lapped up the blood and snarled like a kitten as he ground tender flesh between his tiny teeth. Thor, as in all his food-seeking, hunted first for the tidbits, though the *sapoos oowin* had made him as empty as a room without furniture. He pulled out the thin leafs of fat from about the kidneys and bowels, and munched at yard-long strings of it, his eyes half closed.

The last of the sun faded away from the mountains, and darkness followed swiftly after the twilight. It was dark when they finished, and little Muskwa was as wide as he was long.

Thor was the greatest of nature's conservators. With him nothing went to waste that was good to eat, and at the present moment if the old bull caribou had deliberately walked within his reach Thor in all probability would not have killed him. He had food, and his business was to store that food where it would be safe.

He went back to the balsam thicket, but the gorged cub now made no effort to follow him. He was vastly contented, and something told him that Thor would not leave the meat. Ten minutes later Thor verified his judgment by returning. In his huge jaws he caught the caribou at the back of the neck. Then he swung himself partly sidewise and began dragging the carcass toward the timber as a dog might have dragged a ten-pound slab of bacon.

The young bull probably weighed four hundred pounds. Had he weighed eight hundred, or even a thousand, Thor would still have dragged him—but had the carcass weighed that much he would have turned straight around and *backed* with his load.

In the edge of the balsams Thor had already found a hollow in the ground. He thrust the carcass into this hollow, and while Muskwa watched with a great and growing interest, he proceeded to cover it over with dry needles, sticks, a rotting tree butt, and a log. He did not rear himself up and leave his "mark" on a tree as a warning to other bears. He simply nosed round for a bit, and then went out of the timber.

Muskwa followed him now, and he had some trouble in properly navigating himself under the handicap of his added weight. The stars were beginning to fill the sky, and under these stars Thor struck straight up a steep and rugged slope that led to the mountaintops. Up and up he went, higher than Muskwa had ever been. They crossed a patch of snow. And then they came to a place where it seemed as if a volcano had disrupted the bowels of a mountain. Man could hardly have traveled where Thor led Muskwa.

At last he stopped. He was on a narrow ledge, with a perpendicular wall of rock at his back. Under him fell away the chaos of torn-up rock and shale. Far below the valley lay a black and bottomless pit.

Thor lay down, and for the first time since his hurt in the other valley he stretched out his head between his great arms, and heaved a deep and restful sigh. Muskwa crept up close to him, so close that he was warmed by Thor's body; and together they slept the deep and peaceful sleep of full stomachs, while over them the stars grew brighter, and the moon came up to flood the peaks and the valley in a golden splendor.

CHAPTER
SEVEN

LANGDON and Bruce crossed the summit into the westward valley in the afternoon of the day Thor left the clay wallow. It was two o'clock when Bruce turned back for the three horses, leaving Langdon on a high ridge to scour the surrounding country through his glasses. For two hours after the packer returned with the outfit they followed slowly along the creek above which the grizzly had traveled, and when they camped for the night they were still two or three miles from the spot where Thor came upon Muskwa. They had not yet found his tracks in the sand of the creek-bottom. Yet Bruce was confident. He knew that Thor had been following the crests of the slopes.

"If you go back out of this country an' write about bears, don't make a fool o' yo'rself like most of the writin' fellows, Jimmy," he said, as they sat back to smoke their pipes after supper. "Two years ago I took a natcherlist out for a month, an' he was so tickled he said 'e'd send me a bunch o' books about bears an' wild things. He did! I read 'em. I laughed at first, an' then I got mad an' made a fire of 'em. Bears is cur'ous. There's a mighty lot of interestin' things to say about 'em without making a fool o' yo'rself. There sure is!"

Langdon nodded.

"One has to hunt and kill and hunt and kill for years before he discovers the real pleasure in big game stalking," he said slowly, looking into the fire. "And when he comes down to that real pleasure, the part of it that absorbs him heart and soul, he finds that after all the big thrill isn't in killing, but in letting live. I want this grizzly, and I'm going to have him. I won't leave the mountains until I kill him. But, on the other hand, we could have killed two other bears today, and I didn't take a shot. I'm learning the game, Bruce— I'm beginning to taste the real pleasure of hunting. And when one hunts in the right way one learns facts. You needn't worry. I'm going to put only facts in what I write."

Suddenly he turned and looked at Bruce.

"What were some of the 'fool things' you read in those books?" he asked.

Bruce blew out a cloud of smoke reflectively.

"What made me maddest," he said, "was what those writer fellows said about bears havin' 'marks.' Good Lord, accordin' to what they said all a bear has to do is stretch 'imself up, put a mark on a tree, and that country is his'n until a bigger bear comes along an' licks 'im. In one book I remember where a grizzly rolled a log up under a tree so he could stand on it an' put his mark above another grizzly's mark. Think of that!

"No bear makes a mark that means anything. I've seen grizzlies bite hunks out o' trees an' scratch 'em just as a cat might, an' in the summer when they get itchy an' begin to lose their hair they stand up an' rub against trees. They rub because they itch an' not because they're leavin' their cards for other bears. Caribou an' moose an' deer do the same thing to get the velvet off their horns.

"Them same writers think every grizzly has his own range, an' they don't—not by a long shot they don't! I've seen eight full-grown grizzlies feedin' on the same slide! You remember, two years ago, we shot four grizzlies in a little valley that wasn't a mile long. Now an' then there's a boss among grizzlies, like this fellow we're after, but even he ain't got his range alone. I'll bet there's twenty other bears in these two valleys! An' that natcherlist I had two years ago couldn't tell a grizzly's track from a black bear's track, an' so 'elp me if he knew what a cinnamon was!"

He took his pipe from his mouth and spat truculently into the fire, and Langdon knew that other things were coming. His richest hours were those when the usually silent Bruce fell into these moods.

"A cinnamon!" he growled. "Think of that, Jimmy— he thought there were such a thing as a cinnamon bear! An' when I told him there wasn't, an' that the cinnamon bear you read about is a black or a grizzly of a cinnamon color, he laughed at me—an' there I was born an' brung up among bears! His eyes fair popped when I told him about the color o' bears, an' he thought I was feedin' him rope. I figgered afterward mebby that was why he sent me the books. He wanted to show me he was right.

"Jimmy, there ain't anything on earth that's got more colors than a bear! I've seen black bears as white as snow, an' I've seen grizzlies almost as black as a black bear. I've seen cinnamon black bears an' I've seen browns an' golds an' almost-yellows of both kinds. They're as different in color as they are in their natchurs an' way of eatin'.

"I figger most natcherlists go out an' get acquainted with one grizzly, an' then they write up all grizzlies accordin' to that one. That ain't fair to the grizzlies, darned if it is! There wasn't one of them books that didn't say the grizzly wasn't the fiercest, man-eatingest cuss alive. He ain't—unless you corner 'im. He's as cur'ous as a kid, an' he's good-natured if you don't bother 'im. Most of 'em are vegetarians, but some of 'em ain't. I've seen grizzlies pull down goat an' sheep an' caribou, an' I've seen other grizzlies feed on the same slides with them animals an' never make a move toward them. They're cur'ous, Jimmy. There's lots you can say about 'em without makin' a fool o' yourself!"

Bruce beat the ash out of his pipe as an emphasis to his final remark. As he reloaded with fresh tobacco, Langdon said:

"You can make up your mind this big fellow we are after is a game-killer, Bruce."

"You can't tell," replied Bruce. "Size don't always tell. I knew a grizzly once that wasn't much bigger'n a dog, an' he was a game-killer. Hundreds of animals are winter-killed in these mount'ins every year, an' when spring comes the bears eat the carcasses; but old flesh don't make game-killers. Sometimes it's born in a grizzly to be a killer, an' sometimes he becomes a killer by chance. If he kills once, he'll kill again.

"Once I was on the side of a mount'in an' saw a goat walk straight into the face of a grizzly. The bear wasn't going to make a move, but the goat was so scared it ran plump into the old fellow, and he killed it. He acted mighty surprised for ten minutes afterward, an' he sniffed an' nosed around the warm carcass for half an hour before he tore it open. That was his first taste of what you might call live game. I didn't kill him, an' I'm sure from that day on he was a big-game hunter."

"I should think size would have something to do with it," argued Langdon. "It seems to me that a bear that eats flesh would be bigger and stronger than if he was a vegetarian."

"That's one o' the cur'ous things you want to write about," replied Bruce, with one of his odd chuckles. "Why is it a bear gets so fat he can hardly walk along in September when he don't feed on much else but berries an' ants an' grubs? Would you get fat on wild currants?

"An' why does he grow so fast during the four or five months he's denned up an' dead to the world without a mouthful to eat or drink?

"Why is it that for a month, an' sometimes two months, the mother gives her cubs milk while she's still what you might call asleep? Her nap ain't much more'n two-thirds over when the cubs are born.

"And why ain't them cubs bigger'n they are? That natcherlist laughed until I thought he'd split when I told him a grizzly bear cub wasn't much bigger'n a house-cat kitten when born!"

"He was one of the few fools who aren't willing to learn—and yet you cannot blame him altogether," said Langdon. "Four or five years ago I wouldn't have believed it, Bruce. I couldn't actually believe it until we dug out those cubs up the Athabasca—one weighed eleven ounces and the other nine. You remember?"

"An' they were a week old, Jimmy. An' the mother weighed eight hundred pounds."

For a few moments they both puffed silently on their pipes.

"Almost—inconceivable," said Langdon then. "And yet it's true. And it isn't a freak of nature, Bruce— it's simply a result of Nature's farsightedness. If the cubs were as large comparatively as a house-cat's kittens the mother-bear could not sustain them during those weeks when she eats and drinks nothing herself. There seems to be just one flaw in this scheme: an ordinary black bear is only about half as large as a grizzly, yet a black bear cub when born is much larger than a grizzly cub. Now why the devil that should be—"

Bruce interrupted his friend with a good-natured laugh.

"That's easy—easy, Jimmy!" he exclaimed. "Do you remember last year when we picked strawberries in the valley an' threw snowballs two hours later up on the mountain? Higher you climb the colder it gets, don't it? Right now—first day of July—you'd half freeze up on some of those peaks! A grizzly dens high, Jimmy, and a black bear dens low. When the snow is four feet deep up where the grizzly dens, the black bear can still feed in the deep valleys an' thick timber. He goes to bed mebby a week or two weeks later than the grizzly, an' he gets up in the spring a week or two weeks earlier; he's fatter when he dens up an' he ain't so poor when he comes out—an' so the mother's got more strength to give to her cubs. It looks that way to me."

"You've hit the nail on the head as sure as you're a year old!" cried Langdon enthusiastically. "Bruce, I never thought of that!"

"There's a good many things you don't think about until you run across 'em," said the mountaineer. "It's what you said a while ago—such things are what makes huntin' a fine sport when you've learned huntin' ain't always killin'—but lettin' live. One day I lay seven hours on a mountaintop watchin' a band o' sheep at play, an' I had more fun than if I'd killed the whole bunch."

Bruce rose to his feet and stretched himself, an after-supper operation that always preceded his announcement that he was going to turn in.

"Fine day tomorrow," he said, yawning. "Look how white the snow is on the peaks."

"Bruce—"

"What?"

"How heavy is this bear we're after?"

"Twelve hundred pounds—mebby a little more. I didn't have the pleasure of lookin' at him so close as you did, Jimmy. If I had we'd been dryin' his skin now!"

"And he's in his prime!"

"Between eight and twelve years old, I'd say, by the way he went up the slope. An old bear don't roll so easy."

"You've run across some pretty old bears, Bruce?"

"So old some of 'em needed crutches," said Bruce, unlacing his boots. "I've shot bears so old they'd lost their teeth."

"How old?"

"Thirty—thirty-five—mebby forty years. Good night, Jimmy!"

"Good night, Bruce!"

Langdon was awakened sometime hours later by a deluge of rain that brought him out of his blankets with a yell to Bruce. They had not put up their tepee, and a moment later he heard Bruce anathematizing their idiocy. The night was as black as a cavern, except when it was broken by lurid flashes of lightning, and the mountains rolled and rumbled with deep thunder. Disentangling himself from his drenched blanket, Langdon stood up. A glare of lightning revealed Bruce sitting in his blankets, his hair dripping down over his long, lean face, and at sight of him Langdon laughed outright.

"Fine day tomorrow," he taunted, repeating Bruce's words of a few hours before. "Look how white the snow is on the peaks!"

Whatever Bruce said was drowned in a crash of thunder.

Langdon waited for another lightning flash and then dove for the shelter of a thick balsam. Under this he crouched for five or ten minutes, when the rain stopped as suddenly as it had begun. The thunder rolled southward, and the lightning went with it. In the darkness he heard Bruce fumbling somewhere near. Then a match was lighted, and he saw his comrade looking at his watch.

"Pretty near three o'clock," he said. "Nice shower, wasn't it?"

"I rather expected it," replied Langdon carelessly. "You know, Bruce, whenever the snow on the peaks is so white—"

"Shut up—an' let's get a fire! Good thing we had sense enough to cover our grub with the blankets. Are yo' wet?"

Langdon was wringing the water from his hair. He felt like a drowned rat.

"No. I was under a thick balsam, and prepared for it. When you called my attention to the whiteness of the snow on the peaks I knew—"

"Forget the snow," growled Bruce, and Langdon could hear him breaking off dry pitch-filled twigs under a spruce.

He went to help him, and five minutes later they had a fire going. The light illumined their faces, and each saw that the other was not unhappy. Bruce was grinning under his sodden hair.

"I was dead asleep when it came," he explained. "An' I thought I'd fallen in a lake. I woke up tryin' to swim."

An early July rain at three o'clock in the morning

in the northern British Columbia mountains is not as warm as it might be, and for the greater part of an hour Langdon and Bruce continued to gather fuel and dry their blankets and clothing. It was five o'clock before they had breakfast, and a little after six when they started with their two saddles and single pack up the valley. Bruce had the satisfaction of reminding Langdon that his prediction had come true, for a glorious day followed the thunder shower.

Under them the meadows were dripping. The valley purred louder with the music of the swollen streamlets. From the mountaintops a half of last night's snow was gone, and to Langdon the flowers seemed taller and more beautiful. The air that drifted through the valley was laden with the sweetness and freshness of the morning, and over and through it all the sun shone in a warm and golden sea.

They headed up the creek-bottom, bending over from their saddles to look at every strip of sand they passed for tracks. They had not gone a quarter of a mile when Bruce gave a sudden exclamation, and stopped. He pointed to a round patch of sand in which Thor had left one of his huge footprints. Langdon dismounted and measured it.

"It's he!" he cried, and there was a thrill of excitement in his voice. "Hadn't we better go without the horses, Bruce?"

The mountaineer shook his head. But before he voiced an opinion he got down from his horse and scanned the sides of the mountains ahead of them through his long telescope. Langdon used his double-barreled hunting glass. They discovered nothing.

"He's still in the creek-bottom, an' he's probably three or four miles ahead," said Bruce. "We'll ride on a couple o' miles an' find a place good for the horses. The grass an' bushes will be dry then."

It was easy to follow Thor's course after this, for he had hung close to the creek. Within three or four hundred yards of the great mass of boulders where the grizzly had come upon the tan-faced cub was a small copse of spruce in the heart of a grassy dip, and here the hunters stripped and hobbled their horses. Twenty minutes later they had come up cautiously to the soft carpet of sand where Thor and Muskwa had become acquainted. The heavy rain had obliterated the cub's tiny footprints, but the sand was cut up by the grizzly's tracks. The packer's teeth gleamed as he looked at Langdon.

"He ain't very far," he whispered. "Shouldn't wonder if he spent the night pretty close an' he's mooshing on just ahead of us."

He wet a finger and held it above his head to get the wind. He nodded significantly.

"We'd better get up on the slopes," he said.

They made their way around the end of the boulders, holding their guns in readiness, and headed for a small coulee that promised an easy ascent of the first slope. At the mouth of this both paused again. Its bottom was covered with sand, and in this sand were the tracks of another bear. Bruce dropped on his knees.

"It's another grizzly," said Langdon.

"No, it ain't; it's a black," said Bruce. "Jimmy, can't I ever knock into yo'r head the difference between a black an' a grizzly track? This is the hind foot, an' the heel is round. If it was a grizzly it would be pointed. An' it's too broad an' clubby f'r a grizzly, an' the claws are too long f'r the length of the foot. It's a black as plain as the nose on yo'r face!"

"And going our way," said Langdon. "Come on!"

Two hundred yards up the coulee the bear had climbed out on the slope. Langdon and Bruce followed. In the thick grass and hard shale of the first crest of the slope the tracks were quickly lost, but the hunters were not much interested in these tracks now. From the height at which they were traveling they had a splendid view below them.

Not once did Bruce take his eyes from the creek-bottom. He knew that it was down there they would find the grizzly, and he was interested in nothing else just at present. Langdon, on the other hand, was interested in everything that might be living or moving about them; every mass of rock and thicket of thorn held possibilities for him, and his eyes were questing the higher ridges and the peaks as well as their immediate trail. It was because of this that he saw something which made him suddenly grip his companion's arm and pull him down beside him on the ground.

"Look!" he whispered, stretching out an arm.

From his kneeling posture Bruce stared. His eyes fairly popped in amazement. Not more than thirty feet above them was a big rock shaped like a dry-goods box, and protruding from behind the farther side of this rock was the rear half of a bear. It was a black bear, its glossy coat shining in the sunlight. For a full half minute Bruce continued to stare. Then he grinned.

"Asleep—dead asleep! Jimmy—you want to see some fun?"

He put down his gun and drew out his long hunting knife. He chuckled softly as he felt of its keen point.

"If you never saw a bear run yo'r goin' to see one run now, Jimmy! You stay here!"

He began crawling slowly and quietly up the slope toward the rock, while Langdon held his breath in anticipation of what was about to happen. Twice Bruce looked back, and he was grinning broadly. There was undoubtedly going to be a very much astonished bear racing for the tops of the Rocky Mountains in another moment or two, and between this thought and the picture of Bruce's long lank figure snaking its way upward foot by foot the humor of the situation fell upon Langdon. Finally Bruce reached the rock. The long knife-blade gleamed in the sun; then it shot forward and a half inch of steel buried itself in the bear's rump. What followed in the next thirty seconds Langdon would never forget. The bear made no movement. Bruce jabbed again. Still there was no movement, and at the second thrust Bruce remained as motionless as the rock against which he was crouching, and his mouth was wide open as he stared down at Langdon.

"Now what the devil do you think of that?" he said, and rose slowly to his feet. "He ain't asleep—he's dead!"

Langdon ran up to him, and they went around the

end of the rock. Bruce still held the knife in his hand and there was an odd expression in his face—a look that put troubled furrows between his eyes as he stood for a moment without speaking.

"I never see anything like that before," he said, slowly sliping his knife in its sheath. "It's a she-bear, an' she had cubs—pretty young cubs, too, from the looks o' her.

"She was after a whistler, and undermined the rock," added Langdon. "Crushed to death, eh, Bruce?"

Bruce nodded.

"I never see anything like it before," he repeated. "I've wondered why they didn't get killed by diggin' under the rocks—but I never see it. Wonder where the cubs are? Poor little devils!"

He was on his knees examing the dead mother's teats.

"She didn't have more'n two—mebby one," he said, rising. "About three months old."

"And they'll starve?"

"If there was only one he probably will. The little cuss had so much milk he didn't have to forage for himself. Cubs is a good deal like babies—you can wean 'em early or you can ha'f grow 'em on pap. An' this is what comes of runnin' off an' leavin' your babies alone," moralized Bruce. "If you ever git married, Jimmy, don't you let yo'r wife do it. Sometimes th' babies burn up or break their necks!"

Again he turned along the crest of the slope, his eyes once more searching the valley, and Langdon followed a step behind him, wondering what had become of the cub.

And Muskwa, still slumbering on the rock-ledge with Thor, was dreaming of the mother who lay crushed under the rock on the slope, and as he dreamed he whimpered softly.

CHAPTER
EIGHT

THE ledge where Thor and Muskwa lay caught the first gleams of the morning sun, and as the sun rose higher the ledge grew warmer and warmer, and Thor, when he awoke, merely stretched himself and made no effort to rise. After his wounds and the *sapoos oowin* and the feast in the valley he was feeling tremendously fine and comfortable, and he was in no very great haste to leave this golden pool of sunlight. For a long time he looked steadily and curiously at Muskwa. In the chill of the night the little cub had snuggled up close between the warmth of Thor's huge forearms, and still lay there, whimpering in his babyish way as he dreamed.

After a time Thor did something that he had never been guilty of before—he sniffed gently at the soft little ball between his paws, and just once his big flat red tongue touched the cub's face; and Muskwa, perhaps still dreaming of his mother, snuggled closer. As little children have won the hearts of savages who were

75

about to slay them, so Muskwa had come strangely into the life of Thor.

The big grizzly was still puzzled. Not only was he struggling against an unaccountable dislike of all cubs in general, but also against the firmly established habits of ten years of aloneness. Yet he was beginning to comprehend that there was something very pleasant and companionable in the nearness of Muskwa. With the coming of man a new emotion had entered into his being—perhaps only the spark of an emotion. Until one has enemies, and faces dangers, one cannot fully appreciate friendship—and it may be that Thor, who now confronted real enemies and a real danger for the first time, was beginning to understand what friendship meant. Also it was drawing near to his mating season, and about Muskwa was the scent of his mother. And so as Muskwa continued to bask and dream in the sunshine, there was a growing content in Thor.

He looked down into the valley, shimmering in the wet of the night's rain, and he saw nothing to rouse discontent; he sniffed the air, and it was filled with the unpolluted sweetness of growing grass, of flowers, and balsam, and water fresh from the clouds.

Thor began to lick his wound, and it was this movement that roused Muskwa. The cub lifted his head. He blinked at the sun for a moment—then rubbed his face sleepily with his tiny paw and stood up. Like all youngsters, he was ready for another day, in spite of the hardships and toil of the preceding one.

While Thor still lay restfully looking down into the valley, Muskwa began investigating the crevices in the rock wall, and tumbled about among the boulders on the ledge.

From the valley Thor turned his eyes to the cub. There was curiosity in his attitude as he watched Muskwa's antics and queer tumblings among the rocks. Then he rose cumbrously and shook himself.

For at least five minutes he stood looking down into the valley, and sniffing the wind, as motionless as though carven out of rock. And Muskwa, perking up his little ears, came and stood beside him, his sharp little eyes peering from Thor off into sunlit space, and then back to Thor again, as if wondering what was about to happen next.

The big grizzly answered the question. He turned along the rock shelf and began descending into the valley. Muskwa tagged behind, just as he had followed the day before. The cub felt twice as big and fully twice as strong as yesterday, and he no longer was obsessed by that uncomfortable yearning for his mother's milk. Thor had graduated him quickly, and he was a meat-eater. And he knew they were returning to where they had feasted last night.

They had descended half the distance of the slope when the wind brought something to Thor. A deep-chested growl rolled out of him as he stopped for a moment, the thick ruff about his neck bristling ominously. The scent he had caught came from the direction of his cache, and it was an odor which he was not in a humor to tolerate in this particular locality. Strongly he smelled the presence of another bear. This would not have excited him under ordinary conditions, and it would not have excited him now had the presence been that of a female bear. But the scent was that of a he-bear, and it drifted strongly up a rock-cut ravine that ran straight down toward the balsam patch in which he had hidden the caribou.

Thor stopped to ask himself no questions. Growling under his breath, he began to descend so swiftly that Muskwa had great difficulty in keeping up with him. Not until they came to the edge of the plain that overlooked the lake and the balsams did they stop. Muskwa's little jaws hung open as he panted. Then his ears pricked forward, he stared, and suddenly every muscle in his small body became rigid.

Seventy-five yards below them their cache was being outraged. The robber was a huge black bear. He was a splendid outlaw. He was, perhaps, three hundred pounds lighter than Thor, but he stood almost as high, and in the sunlight his coat shone with the velvety gloss of sable—the biggest and boldest bear that had entered Thor's domains in many a day. He had pulled the caribou carcass from its hiding-place and was eating as Thor and Muskwa looked down on him.

After a moment Muskwa peered up questioningly at Thor. "What are we going to do?" he seemed to ask. "He's got our dinner!"

Slowly and very deliberately Thor began picking his way down those last seventy-five yards. He seemed to be in no hurry now.

When he reached the edge of the meadow, perhaps thirty or forty yards form the big invader, he stopped again. There was nothing particularly ugly in his attitude, but the ruff about his shoulders was bigger than Muskwa had ever seen it before.

The black looked up from his feast, and for a full half minute they eyed each other. In a slow, pendulumlike motion the grizzly's huge head swung from side to side; the black was motionless as a sphinx.

Four or five feet from Thor stood Muskwa. In a small-boyish sort of way he knew that something was going to happen soon, and in that same small-boyish way he was ready to put his stub of a tail between his legs and flee with Thor, or advance and fight with him. His eyes were curiously attracted by that pendulumlike swing of Thor's head. All nature understood that swing. Man had learned to understand it. "Look out when a grizzly rolls his head!" is the first commandment of the bear-hunter in the mountains.

The big black understood, and like other bears in Thor's domain, he should have slunk a little backward, turned about and made his exit. Thor gave him ample time. But the black was a new bear in the valley—and he was not only that: he was a powerful bear, and unwhipped; and he had overlorded a range of his own. He stood his ground.

The first growl of menace that passed between the two came from the black.

Again Thor advanced, slowly and deliberately—straight for the robber. Muskwa followed halfway and then stopped and squatted himself on his belly. Ten feet from the carcass Thor paused again; and now his huge head swung more swiftly back and forth, and a low rumbling thunder came from between his half-open jaws. The black's ivory fangs snarled; Muskwa whined.

Again Thor advanced, a foot at a time, and now his

gaping jaws almost touched the ground, and his huge body was hunched low.

When no more than the length of a yardstick separated them there came a pause. For perhaps thirty seconds they were like two angry men, each trying to strike terror to the other's heart by the steadiness of his look.

Muskwa shook as if with the ague, and whined—softly and steadily he whined, and the whine reached Thor's ears. What happened after that began so quickly that Muskwa was struck dumb with terror, and he lay flattened out on the earth as motionless as a stone.

With that grinding, snarling grizzly roar, which is unlike any other animal cry in the world, Thor flung himself at the black. The black reared a little—just enough to fling himself backward easily as they came together breast to breast. He rolled upon his back, but Thor was too old a fighter to be caught by that first vicious ripping stroke of the black's hind foot, and he buried his four long flesh-rending teeth to the bone of his enemy's shoulder. At the same time he struck a terrific cutting stroke with his left paw.

Thor was a digger, and his claws were dulled; the black was not a digger, but a tree-climber, and his claws were like knives. And like knives they buried themselves in Thor's wounded shoulder, and the blood spurted forth afresh.

With a roar that seemed to set the earth trembling, the huge grizzly lunged backward and reared himself to his full nine feet. He had given the black warning. Even after their first tussle his enemy might have retreated and he would not have pursued. Now it was a fight to the death! The black had done more than ravage his cache. He had opened the man-wound!

A minute before Thor had been fighting for law and right—without great animosity or serious desire to kill. Now, however, he was terrible. His mouth was open, and it was eight inches from jaw to jaw; his lips were drawn up until his white teeth and his red gums were bared; muscles stood out like cords on his nostrils, and between his eyes was a furrow like the cleft made by an ax in the trunk of a pine. His eyes shone with the glare of red garnets, their greenish-black pupils almost obliterated by the ferocious fire that was in them. Man, facing Thor in this moment, would have known that only one would come out alive.

Thor was not a "stand-up" fighter. For perhaps six or seven seconds he remained erect, but as the black advanced a step he dropped quickly to all fours.

The black met him halfway, and after this—for many minutes—Muskwa hugged closer and closer to the earth while with gleaming eyes he watched the battle. It was such a fight as only the jungles and the mountains see, and the roar of it drifted up and down the valley.

Like human creatures the two giant beasts used their powerful forearms while with fangs and hind feet they ripped and tore. For two minutes they were in a close and deadly embrace, both rolling on the ground, now one under and then the other. The black clawed ferociously; Thor used chiefly his teeth and his terrible right hind foot. With his forearms he made no effort to rend the black, but used them to hold and throw his enemy. He was fighting to get *under*, as he had flung himself under the caribou he had disemboweled.

Again and again Thor buried his long fangs in the other's flesh; but in fang-fighting the black was even quicker than he, and his right shoulder was being literally torn to pieces when their jaws met in midair. Muskwa heard the clash of them; he heard the grind of teeth on teeth, the sickening crunch of bone.

Then suddenly the black was flung upon his side as though his neck had been broken, and Thor was at his throat. Still the black fought, his gaping and bleeding jaws powerless now as the grizzly closed his own huge jaws on the jugular.

Muskwa stood up. He was shivering still, but with a new and strange emotion. This was not play, as he and his mother had played. For the first time he was looking upon *battle*, and the thrill of it sent the blood hot and fast through his little body. With a faint, puppyish snarl he darted in. His teeth sank futilely into the thick hair and tough hide of the black's rump. He pulled and he snarled; he braced himself with his forefeet and tugged at his mouthful of hair, filled with a blind and unaccountable rage.

The black twisted himself upon his back, and one of his hind feet raked Thor from chest to vent. That stroke would have disemboweled a caribou or a deer; it left a red, open, bleeding wound three feet long on Thor.

Before it could be repeated, the grizzly swung himself sidewise, and the second blow caught Muskwa. The flat of the black's foot struck him, and for twenty feet he was sent like a stone out of a slingshot. He was not cut, but he was stunned.

In that same moment Thor released his hold on his enemy's throat, and swung two or three feet to one side. He was dripping blood. The black's shoulders, chest, and neck were saturated with it; huge chunks had been torn from his body. He made an effort to rise, and Thor was on him again.

This time Thor got his deadliest of all holds. His great jaws clamped in a death-grip over the upper part of the black's nose. One terrific grinding crunch, and the fight was over. The black could not have lived after that. But this fact Thor did not know. It was now easy for him to rip with those knifelike claws on his hind feet. He continued to maul and tear for ten minutes after the black was dead.

When Thor finally quit the scene of battle was terrible to look upon. The ground was torn up and red; it was covered with great strips of black hide and pieces of flesh; and the black, on the under side, was torn open from end to end.

Two miles away, tense and white and scarcely breathing as they looked through their glasses, Langdon and Bruce crouched beside a rock on the mountainside. At that distance they had witnessed the terrific spectacle, but they could not see the cub. As Thor stood panting and bleeding over his lifeless enemy, Langdon lowered his glass.

"My God!" he breathed.

Bruce sprang to his feet.

"Come on!" he cried. "The black's dead! If we hustle we can get our grizzly!"

And down in the meadow Muskwa ran to Thor with a bit of warm black hide in his mouth, and Thor lowered his great bleeding head, and just once his red tongue shot out and caressed Muskwa's face. For the little tan-faced cub had proved himself; and it may be that Thor had seen and understood.

CHAPTER
NINE

NEITHER Thor nor Muskwa went near the caribou meat after the big fight. Thor was in no condition to eat, and Muskwa was so filled with excitement and trembling that he could not swallow a mouthful. He continued to worry a strip of black hide, snarling and growling in his puny way, as though finishing what the other had begun.

For many minutes the grizzly stood with his big head drooping, and the blood gathered in splashes under him. He was facing down the valley. There was almost no wind—so little that it was scarcely possible to tell from which direction it came. Eddies of it were caught in the coulees, and higher up about the shoulders and peaks it blew stronger. Now and then one of these higher movements of air would sweep gently downward and flow through the valley for a few moments in a great noiseless breath that barely stirred the tops of the balsams and spruce. One of these mountain-breaths came as Thor faced the east. And with it, faint and terrible, came the *man-smell*!

Thor roused himself with a sudden growl from the lethargy into which he had momentarily allowed himself to sink. His relaxed muscles hardened. He raised his head and sniffed the wind.

Muskwa ceased his futile fight with the bit of hide and also sniffed the air. It was warm with the man-scent, for Langdon and Bruce were running and sweating, and the odor of man-sweat drifts heavy and far. It filled Thor with a fresh rage. For a second time it came when he was hurt and bleeding. He had already associated the man-smell with hurt, and now it was doubly impressed upon him. He turned his head and snarled at the mutilated body of the big black. Then he snarled menacingly in the face of the wind. He was in no humor to run away. In these moments, if Bruce and Langdon had appeared over the rise, Thor would have charged with that deadly ferocity which lead can scarcely stop, and which has given to his kind their terrible name.

But the breath of air passed, and there followed a peaceful calm. The valley was filled with the purr of running water; from their rocks the whistlers called forth their soft notes; up on the green plain the ptarmigan were fluting, and rising in white-winged flocks. These things soothed Thor, as a woman's gentle hand quiets an angry man. For five minutes he continued to rumble and growl as he tried vainly to catch the scent again; but the rumbling and growling grew steadily less, and finally he turned and walked slowly toward the coulee down which he and Muskwa had come a little while before. Muskwa followed.

The coulee, or ravine, hid them from the valley as

they ascended. Its bottom was covered with rock and shale. The wounds Thor had received in the fight, unlike bullet wounds, had stopped bleeding after the first few minutes, and he left no telltale red spots behind. The ravine took them to the first chaotic up-heaval of rock halfway up the mountain, and here they were still more lost to view from below.

They stopped and drank at a pool formed by the melting snow on the peaks, and then went on. Thor did not stop when they reached the ledge on which they had slept the previous night. And this time Muskwa was not tired when they reached the ledge. Two days had made a big change in the little tan-faced cub. He was not so round and puffy. And he was stronger—a great deal stronger; he was becoming hardened, and under Thor's strenuous tutelage he was swiftly graduating from cubhood to young bear-hood.

It was evident that Thor had followed this ledge at some previous time. He knew where he was going. It continued up and up, and finally seemed to end in the face of a precipitous wall of rock. Thor's trail led him directly to a great crevice, hardly wider than his body, and through this he went, emerging at the edge of the wildest and roughest slide of rock that Muskwa had ever seen. It looked like a huge quarry, and it broke through the timber far below them, and reached almost to the top of the mountain above.

For Muskwa to make his way over the thousand pitfalls of that chaotic upheaval was an impossibility, and as Thor began to climb over the first rocks the cub stopped and whined. It was the first time he had given up, and when he saw that Thor gave no attention to his whine, terror seized upon him and he cried for help as loudly as he could while he hunted frantically for a path up through the rocks.

Utterly oblivious of Muskwa's predicament, Thor continued until he was fully thirty yards away. Then he stopped, faced about deliberately, and waited.

This gave Muskwa courage, and he scratched and clawed and even used his chin and teeth in his efforts to follow. It took him ten minutes to reach Thor, and he was completely winded. Then, all at once, his terror vanished. For Thor stood on a white, narrow path that was as solid as a floor.

The path was perhaps eighteen inches wide. It was unusual- and mysterious-looking, and strangely out of place where it was. It looked as though an army of workmen had come along with hammers and had broken up tons of sandstone and slate, and then filled in between the boulders with rubble, making a smooth and narrow road that in places was ground to the fineness of powder and the hardness of cement. But instead of hammers, the hoofs of a hundred or perhaps a thousand generations of mountain sheep had made the trail. It was the sheep-path over the range. The first band of bighorn may have blazed the way before Columbus discovered America; surely it had taken a great many years for hoofs to make that smooth road among the rocks.

Thor used the path as one of his highways from valley to valley, and there were other creatures of the mountains who used it as well as he, and more frequently. As he stood waiting for Muskwa to get his wind they both heard an odd chuckling sound approaching them from above. Forty or fifty feet up the slide the path twisted and descended a little depression behind a huge boulder, and out from behind this boulder came a big porcupine.

There is a law throughout the North that a man shall not kill a porcupine. He is the "lost man's friend," for the wandering and starving prospector or hunter can nearly always find a porcupine, if nothing else; and a child can kill him. He is the humorist of the wilderness—the happiest, the best-natured, and altogether the mildest-mannered beast that ever drew breath. He talks and chatters and chuckles incessantly, and when he travels he walks like a huge animated pincushion; he is oblivious of everything about him as though asleep.

As this particular "porky" advanced upon Muskwa and Thor, he was communing happily with himself, the chuckling notes he made sounding very much like a baby's cooing. He was enormously fat, and as he waddled slowly along his side and tail quills clicked on the stones. His eyes were on the path at his feet. He was deeply absorbed in nothing at all, and he was within five feet of Thor before he saw the grizzly. Then, in a wink, he humped himself into a ball. For a few seconds he scolded vociferously. After that he was as silent as a sphinx, his little red eyes watching the big bear.

Thor did not want to kill him, but the path was narrow, and he was ready to go on. He advanced a foot or two, and Porky turned his back toward Thor and made ready to deliver a swipe with his powerful tail. In that tail were several hundred quills. As Thor had more than once come into contact with porcupine quills, he hesitated.

Muskwa was looking on curiously. He still had his lesson to learn, for the quill he had once picked up in his foot had been a loose quill. But since the porcupine seemed to puzzle Thor, the cub turned and made ready to go back along the slide if it became necessary. Thor advanced another foot, and with a sudden *chuck, chuck, chuck*—the most vicious sound he was capable of making—Porky advanced backward and his broad, thick tail whipped through the air with a force that would have driven quills a quarter of an inch into the butt of a tree. Having missed, he humped himself again, and Thor stepped out on the boulder and circled around him. There he waited for Muskwa.

Porky was immensely satisfied with his triumph. He unlimbered himself; his quills settled a bit; and he advanced toward Muskwa, at the same time resuming his good-natured chuckling. Instinctively the cub hugged the edge of the path, and in doing so slipped over the edge. By the time he had scrambled up again Porky was four or five feet beyond him and totally absorbed in his travel.

The adventure of the sheep-trail was not yet quite over, for scarcely had Porky maneuvered himself to safety when around the edge of the big boulder above appeared a badger, hot on the fresh and luscious scent of his favorite dinner, a porcupine. This worthless outlaw of the mountains was three times as large as Muskwa, and every ounce of him was fighting muscle and bone and claw and sharp teeth. He had a white mark on his nose and forehead; his legs were short and thick; his tail was bushy, and the claws on his front feet were almost as long as a bear's. Thor greeted him with an immediate growl of warning, and the badger scooted back up the trail in fear of his life.

Meanwhile Porky lumbered slowly along in quest of new feeding-grounds, talking and singing to himself, forgetting entirely what had happened a minute or two before, and unconscious of the fact that Thor had saved him from a death as certain as though he had fallen over a thousand-foot precipice.

For nearly a mile Thor and Muskwa followed the Bighorn Highway before its winding course brought them at last to the very top of the range. They were fully three-quarters of a mile above the creek-bottom, and so narrow in places was the crest of the mountain along which the sheep-trail led that they could look down into both valleys.

To Muskwa it was all a greenish golden haze below him; the depths seemed illimitable; the forest along the stream was only a black streak, and the parklike clumps of balsams and cedars on the farther slopes looked like very small bosks of thorn or buffalo willow.

Up here the wind was blowing, too. It whipped him with a strange fierceness, and half a dozen times he felt the mysterious and very unpleasant chill of snow under his feet. Twice a great bird swooped near him. It was the biggest bird he had ever seen—an eagle. The second time it came so near that he heard the *beat* of it, and saw its great, fierce head and lowering talons.

Thor whirled toward the eagle and growled. If

Muskwa had been alone, the cub would have gone sailing off in those murderous talons. As it was, the third time the eagle circled it was down the slope from them. It was after other game. The scent of the game came to Thor and Muskwa, and they stopped.

Perhaps a hundred yards below them was a shelving slide of soft shale, and on this shale, basking in the warm sun after their morning's feed lower down, was a band of sheep. There were twenty or thirty of them, mostly ewes and their lambs. Three huge old rams were lying on a patch of snow farther to the east.

With his six-foot wings spread out like twin fans, the eagle continued to circle. He was as silent as a feather floating with the wind. The ewes and even the old bighorns were unconscious of his presence over them. Most of the lambs were lying close to their mothers, but two or three of a livelier turn of mind were wandering over the shale and occasionally hopping about in playful frolic.

The eagle's fierce eyes were upon these youngsters. Suddenly he drifted farther away—a full rifle-shot distance straight in the face of the wind; then he swung gracefully, and came back with the wind. And as he came, his wings apparently motionless, he gathered greater and greater speed, and shot like a rocket straight for the lambs. He seemed to have come and gone like a great shadow, and just one plaintive, agonized bleat marked his passing—and two little lambs were left where there had been three.

There was instant commotion on the slide. The ewes began to run back and forth and bleat excitedly. The three rams sprang up and stood like rocks, their huge battlemented heads held high as they scanned the depths below them and the peaks above for new danger.

One of them saw Thor, and the deep, grating bleat of warning that rattled out of his throat a hunter could have heard a mile away. As he gave his danger signal he started down the slide, and in another moment an avalanche of hoofs was clattering down the steep shale slope, loosening small stones and boulders that went tumbling and crashing down the mountain with a din that steadily increased as they set others in motion on the way. This was all mighty interesting to Muskwa, and he would have stood for a long time looking down for other things to happen if Thor had not led him on.

After a time the Bighorn Highway began to descend into the valley from the upper end of which Thor had been driven by Langdon's first shots. They were now six or eight miles north of the timber in which the hunters had made their permanent camp, and headed for the lower tributaries of the Skeena.

Another hour of travel, and the bare shale and gray crags were above them again, and they were on the green slopes. After the rocks, and the cold winds, and the terrible glare he had seen in the eagle's eyes, the warm and lovely valley into which they were descending lower and lower was a paradise to Muskwa.

It was evident that Thor had something in his mind. He was not rambling now. He cut off the ends and the bulges of the slopes. With his head hunched low he traveled steadily northward, and a compass could not have marked out a straighter line for the lower waters of the Skeena. He was tremendously businesslike, and Muskwa, tagging bravely along behind, wondered if he were never going to stop; if there could be anything in the whole wide world finer for a big grizzly and a little tan-faced cub than these wonderful sunlit slopes which Thor seemed in such great haste to leave.

CHAPTER
TEN

IF IT had not been for Langdon, this day of the
fight between the two bears would have held still
greater excitement and another and deadlier peril
for Thor and Muskwa. Three minutes after the hunters had arrived breathless and sweating upon the
scene of the sanguinary conflict Bruce was ready and
anxious to continue the pursuit of Thor. He knew the
big grizzly could not be far away; he was certain that
Thor had gone up the mountain. He found signs of
the grizzly's feet in the gravel of the coulee at just
about the time Thor and the tan-faced cub struck the
Bighorn Highway.

His arguments failed to move Langdon. Stirred to
the depth of his soul by what he had seen, and what
he saw about him now, the hunter-naturalist refused
to leave the bloodstained and torn-up arena in which
the grizzly and the black had fought their duel.

"If I knew that I was not going to fire a single shot,
I would travel five thousand miles to see this," he said.

"It's worth thinking about, and looking over, Bruce. The grizzly won't spoil. This will—in a few hours. If there's a story here we can dig out I want it."

Again and again Langdon went over the battlefield, noting the ripped-up ground, the big spots of dark-red stain, the strips of flayed skin, and the terrible wounds on the body of the dead black. For half an hour Bruce paid less attention to these things than he did to the carcass of the caribou. At the end of that time he called Langdon to the edge of the clump of balsams.

"You wanted the story," he said, "an' I've got it for you, Jimmy."

He entered the balsams and Langdon followed him. A few steps under the cover Bruce halted and pointed to the hollow in which Thor had cached his meat. The hollow was stained with blood.

"You was right in your guess, Jimmy," he said. "Our grizzly is a meat-eater. Last night he killed a caribou out there in the meadow. I know it was the grizzly that killed 'im an' not the black, because the tracks along the edge of the timber are grizzly tracks. Come on. I'll show you where 'e jumped the caribou!"

He led the way back into the meadow, and pointed out where Thor had dragged down the young bull. There were bits of flesh and a great deal of stain where he and Muskwa had feasted.

"He hid the carcass in the balsams after he had filled himself," went on Bruce. "This morning the black came along, smelled the meat, an' robbed the cache. Then back come the grizzly after his morning feed, an' that's what happened! There's yo'r story, Jimmy."

"And—he may come back again?" asked Langdon.

"Not on your life, he won't!" cried Bruce. "He wouldn't touch that carcass ag'in if he was starving. Just now this place is like poison to him."

After that Bruce left Langdon to meditate alone on the field of battle while he began trailing Thor. In the shade of the balsams Langdon wrote for a steady hour, frequently rising to establish new facts or verify others already discovered. Meanwhile the mountain-eer made his way foot by foot up the coulee. Thor had left no blood, but where others would have seen nothing Bruce detected the signs of his passing. When he returned to where Langdon was completing his notes, his face wore a look of satisfaction.

"He went over the mount'in," he said briefly.

It was noon before they climbed over the volcanic quarry of rock and followed the Bighorn Highway to the point where Thor and Muskwa had watched the eagle and the sheep. They ate their lunch here, and scanned the valley through their glasses. Bruce was silent for a long time. Then he lowered his telescope, and turned to Langdon.

"I guess I've got his range pretty well figgered out," he said. "He runs these two valleys, an' we've got our camp too far south. See that timber down there? That's where our camp should be. What do you say to goin' back over the divide with our horses an' moving up here?"

"And leave our grizzly until tomorrow?"

Bruce nodded.

"We can't go after 'im and leave our horses tied up in the creek-bottom back there."

Langdon boxed his glasses and rose to his feet. Suddenly he grew rigid.

"What was that?"

"I didn't hear anything," said Bruce.

For a moment they stood side by side, listening. A gust of wind whistled about their ears. It died away.

"Hear it!" whispered Langdon, and his voice was filled with a sudden excitement.

"The dogs!" cried Bruce.

"Yes, the dogs!"

They leaned forward, their ears turned to the south, and faintly there came to them the distant, thrilling tongue of the Airedales!

Metoosin had come, and he was seeking them in the valley!

CHAPTER
ELEVEN

THOR was on what the Indians call a *pimootao*. His brute mind had all at once added two and two together, and while perhaps he did not make four of it, his mental arithmetic was accurate enough to convince him that straight north was the road to travel.

By the time Langdon and Bruce had reached the summit of the Bighorn Highway, and were listening to the distant tonguing of the dogs, little Muskwa was in abject despair. Following Thor had been like a game of tag with never a moment's rest.

An hour after they left the sheep trail they came to the rise in the valley where the waters separated. From this point one creek flowed southward into the Tacla Lake country and the other northward into the Babine, which was a tributary of the Skeena. They descended very quickly into a much lower country, and for the first time Muskwa encountered marshland, and traveled at times through grass so rank and thick

99

that he could not see but could only hear Thor forging on ahead of him.

The stream grew wider and deeper, and in places they skirted the edges of dark, quiet pools that Muskwa thought must have been of immeasurable depth. These pools gave Muskwa his first breathing-spells. Now and then Thor would stop and sniff over the edge of them. He was hunting for something, and yet he never seemed to find it; and each time that he started on afresh Muskwa was so much nearer to the end of his endurance.

They were fully seven miles north of the point from which Bruce and Langdon were scanning the valley through their glasses when they came to a lake. It was a dark and unfriendly looking lake to Muskwa, who had never seen anything but sunlit pools in the dips. The forest grew close down to its shore. In places it was almost black. Queer birds squawked in the thick reeds. It was heavy with a strange odor—a fragrance of something that made the cub lick his little chops, and filled him with hunger.

For a minute or two Thor stood sniffing this scent that filled the air. It was the smell of fish.

Slowly the big grizzly began picking his way along the edge of the lake. He soon came to the mouth of a small creek. It was not more than twenty feet wide, but it was dark and quiet and deep, like the lake itself. For a hundred yards Thor made his way up this creek, until he came to where a number of trees had fallen across it, forming a jam. Close to this jam the water was covered with a green scum. Thor knew what lay under that scum, and very quietly he crept out on the logs.

Midway in the stream he paused, and with his right paw gently brushed back the scum so that an open pool of clear water lay directly under him.

Muskwa's bright little eyes watched him from the shore. He knew that Thor was after something to eat, but how he was going to get it out of that pool of water puzzled and interested him in spite of his weariness.

Thor stretched himself out on his belly, his head and right paw well over the jam. He now put his paw a foot into the water and held it there very quietly. He could see clearly to the bottom of the stream. For a few moments he saw only this bottom, a few sticks, and the protruding end of a limb. Then a long slim shadow moved slowly under him—a fifteen-inch trout. It was too deep for him, and Thor did not make an excited plunge.

Patiently he waited, and very soon this patience was rewarded. A beautiful red-spotted trout floated out from under the scum, and so suddenly that Muskwa gave a yelp of terror, Thor's huge paw sent a shower of water a dozen feet into the air, and the fish landed with a thump within three feet of the cub. Instantly Muskwa was upon it. His sharp teeth dug into it as it flopped and struggled.

Thor rose on the logs, but when he saw that Muskwa had taken possession of the fish, he resumed his former position. Muskwa was just finishing his first real kill when a second spout of water shot upward and another trout pirouetted shoreward through the air. This time Thor followed quickly, for he was hungry.

It was a glorious feast they had that early afternoon beside the shaded creek. Five times Thor knocked fish out from under the scum, but for the life of him Muskwa could not eat more than his first trout.

For several hours after their dinner they lay in a cool, hidden spot close to the logjam. Muskwa did not sleep soundly. He was beginning to understand that life was now largely a matter of personal responsibility with him, and his ears had begun to attune themselves to sound. Whenever Thor moved or heaved a deep sigh, Muskwa knew it. After that day's marathon with the grizzly he was filled with uneasiness—a fear that he might lose his big friend and food-killer, and he was determined that the parent he had adopted should have no opportunity of slipping away from him unheard and unseen. But Thor had no intention of deserting his little comrade. In fact, he was becoming quite fond of Muskwa.

It was not alone for his hunger for fish or fear of his enemies that was bringing Thor into the lower country of the Babine waterways. For a week past there had been in him a steadily growing unrest, and it had reached its climax in these last two or three days of battle and fight. He was filled with a strange and unsatisfied yearning, and as Muskwa napped in his little bed among the bushes Thor's ears were keenly alert for certain sounds and his nose frequently sniffed the air. He wanted a mate.

It was *puskoowepesim*—the "molting moon"—and always in this moon, or the end of the "egg-laying moon," which was June, he hunted for the female that came to him from the western ranges. He was almost entirely a creature of habit, and always he made this particular detour, entering the other valley again far down toward the Babine. He never failed to feed on fish along the way, and the more fish he ate the stronger was the odor of him. It is barely possible Thor had discovered that this perfume of golden-spotted trout made him more attractive to his ladylove. Anyway, he ate fish, and he smelled abundantly.

Thor rose and stretched himself two hours before sunset, and he knocked three more fish out of the water. Muskwa ate the head of one and Thor finished the rest. Then they continued their pilgrimage.

It was a new world that Muskwa entered now. In it there were none of the old familiar sounds. The purring drone of the upper valley was gone. There were no whistlers, and no ptarmigan, and no fat little gophers running about. The water of the lake lay still, and dark, and deep, with black and sunless pools hiding themselves under the roots of trees, so close did the forest cling to it. There were no rocks to climb over, but dank, soft logs, thick windfalls, and litters of brush. The air was different, too. It was very still. Under their feet at times was a wonderful carpet of soft moss in which Thor sank nearly to his armpits. And the forest was filled with a strange gloom and many mysterious shadows, and there hung heavily in it the pungent smells of decaying vegetation.

Thor did not travel so swiftly here. The silence and the gloom and the oppressively scented air seemed to rouse his caution. He stepped quietly; frequently he stopped and looked about him, and listened; he smelled at the edges of pools hidden under the roots; every new sound brought him to a stop, his head hung low and his ears alert.

Several times Muskwa saw shadowy things floating through the gloom. They were the big gray owls that turned snow white in winter. And once, when it was almost dark, they came upon a pop-eyed, loose-jointed, fierce-looking creature in the trail who scurried away like a ball at sight of Thor. It was a lynx.

It was not yet quite dark when Thor came out very quietly into a clearing, and Muskwa found himself first on the shore of a creek, and then close to a big pond. The air was full of the breath and warmth of a new kind of life. It was not fish, and yet it seemed to come from the pond, in the center of which were three or four circular masses that looked like great brush-heaps plastered with a coating of mud.

Whenever he came into this end of the valley Thor always paid a visit to the beaver colony, and occasionally he helped himself to a fat young beaver for supper or breakfast. This evening he was not hungry, and he was in a hurry. In spite of these two facts he stood for some minutes in the shadows near the pond.

The beavers had already begun their night's work. Muskwa soon understood the significance of the shimmering streaks that ran swiftly over the surface of the water. At the end of each streak was always a dark, flat head, and now he saw that most of these streaks began at the farther edge of the pond and made directly for a long, low barrier that shut in the water a hundred yards to the east.

This particular barrier was strange to Thor, and with his maturer knowledge of beaver ways he knew that his engineering friends—whom he ate only occasionally—were broadening their domain by building a new dam. As they watched, two fat workmen shoved a four-foot length of log into the pond with a big splash, and one of them began piloting it toward the scene of building operations, while his companion returned to other work. A little later there was a crash in the timber on the opposite side of the pond, where another workman had succeeded in felling a tree. Then Thor made his way toward the dam.

Almost instantly there was a terrific crack out in the middle of the pond, followed by a tremendous splash. An old beaver had seen Thor and with the flat side of his broad tail had given the surface of the water a warning slap that cut the still air like a rifle shot. All at once there were splashings and divings in every direction, and a moment later the pond was ruffled and heaving as a score of interrupted workers dove excitedly under the surface to the safety of their brush-ribbed and mud-plastered strongholds, and Muskwa was so absorbed in the general excitement that he almost forgot to follow Thor.

He overtook the grizzly at the dam. For a few moments Thor inspected the new work, and then tested it with his weight. It was solid, and over this bridge ready-built for them they crossed to the higher ground on the opposite side. A few hundred yards farther on Thor struck a fairly well-beaten caribou trail which in the course of half an hour led them around the end of the lake to the outlet stream flowing north.

Every minute Muskwa was hoping that Thor would stop. His afternoon's nap had not taken the lameness out of his legs nor the soreness from the tender pads of his feet. He had had enough, and more than enough, of travel, and could he have regulated the world according to his own wishes he would not have walked another mile for a whole month. Mere walking would not have been so bad, but to keep up with Thor's ambling gait he was compelled to trot, like a stubby four-year-old child hanging desperately to the thumb of a big and fast-walking man. Muskwa had not even a thumb to hang to. The bottoms of his feet were like boils; his tender nose was raw from contact with brush and the knife-edged marsh grass, and his little back felt all caved in. Still he hung on desperately, until the creek-bottom was again sand and gravel, and traveling was easier.

The stars were up now, millions of them, clear and brilliant; and it was quite evident that Thor had set his mind on an "all-night hike," a *kuppatipsk pimootao,* as a Cree tracker would have called it. Just how it would have ended for Muskwa is a matter of conjecture had not the spirits of thunder and rain and lightning put their heads together to give him a rest.

For perhaps an hour the stars were undimmed, and Thor kept on like a heathen without a soul, while Muskwa limped on all four feet. Then a low rumbling gathered in the west. It grew louder and louder, and approached swiftly—straight from the warm Pacific. Thor grew uneasy, and sniffed in the face of it. Livid streaks began to crisscross a huge pall of black that was closing in on them like a vast curtain. The stars began to go out. A moaning wind came. And then the rain.

Thor had found a huge rock that shelved inward, like a lean-to, and he crept back under this with Muskwa before the deluge descended. For many minutes it was more like a flood than a rain. It seemed as though a part of the Pacific Ocean had been scooped up and dropped on them, and in half an hour the creek was a swollen torrent.

The lightning and the crash of thunder terrified Muskwa. Now he could see Thor in great blinding flashes of fire, and the next instant it was as black as pitch; the tops of the mountains seemed falling down into the valley; the earth trembled and shook—and he snuggled closer and closer to Thor until at last he lay between his two forearms, half buried in the long hair of the big grizzly's shaggy chest. Thor himself was not much concerned in these noisy convulsions of nature, except to keep himself dry. When he took a bath he wanted the sun to be shining and a nice warm rock close at hand on which to stretch himself.

For a long time after its first fierce outbreak the rain continued to fall in a gentle shower. Muskwa liked this, and under the sheltering rock, snuggled against Thor, he felt very comfortable and easily fell asleep. Through long hours Thor kept his vigil alone, drowsing now and then, but kept from sound slumber by the restlessness that was in him.

It stopped raining soon after midnight, but it was very dark, the stream was flooding over its bars, and Thor remained under the rock. Muskwa had a splendid sleep.

Day had come when Thor's stirring roused Muskwa. He followed the grizzly out into the open, feeling tremendously better than last night, though his feet were still sore and his body was stiff.

Thor began to follow the creek again. Along this stream there were low flats and many small bayous where grew luxuriantly the tender grass and roots, and especially the slim long-stemmed lilies on which Thor was fond of feeding. But for a thousand-pound grizzly to fill up on such vegetarian dainties as these consumed many hours, if not one's whole time, and Thor considered that he had no time to lose. Thor was a most ardent lover when he loved at all, which was only a few days out of the year; and during these days he twisted his mode of living around so that while the spirit possessed him he no longer existed for the sole purpose of eating and growing fat. For a short time he put aside his habit of living to eat, and ate to live; and poor Muskwa was almost famished before another dinner was forthcoming.

But at last, early in the afternoon, Thor came to a pool which he could not pass. It was not a dozen feet in width, and it was alive with trout. The fish had not been able to reach the lake above, and they had waited too long after the flood season to descend into the deeper waters of the Babine and the Skeena. They had taken refuge in this pool, which was now about to become a death-trap.

At one end the water was two feet deep; at the other end only a few inches. After pondering over this fact for a few moments, the grizzly waded openly into the deepest part, and from the bank above Muskwa saw the shimmering trout darting into the shallower water. Thor advanced slowly, and now, when he stood in less than eight inches of water, the panic-stricken fish one after another tried to escape back into the deeper part of the pool.

Again and again Thor's big right paw swept up great showers of water. The first inundation knocked Muskwa off his feet. But with it came a two-pound trout which the cub quickly dragged out of range and began eating. So agitated became the pool because of the mighty strokes of Thor's paw that the trout completely lost their heads, and no sooner did they reach one end than they turned about and darted for the other. They kept this up until the grizzly had thrown fully a dozen of their number ashore.

So absorbed was Muskwa in his fish, and Thor in his fishing, that neither had noticed a visitor. Both saw him at about the same time, and for fully thirty seconds they stood and stared, Thor in his pool and the cub over his fish, utter amazement robbing them of the power of movement. The visitor was another grizzly, and as coolly as though he had done the fishing himself he began eating the fish which Thor had thrown out! A worse insult or a deadlier challenge could not have been known in the land of Beardom. Even Muskwa sensed that fact. He looked expectantly at Thor. There was going to be another fight, and he licked his little chops in anticipation.

Thor came up out of the pool slowly. On the bank he paused. The grizzlies gazed at each other, the newcomer crunching a fish as he looked. Neither growled. Muskwa perceived no signs of enmity, and then to his increased astonishment Thor began eating a fish within three feet of the interloper!

Perhaps man is the finest of all God's creations, but when it comes to his respect for old age he is no better, and sometimes not as good, as a grizzly bear; for Thor would not rob an old bear, he would not fight an old bear, and he would not drive an old bear from his own meat—which is more than can be said of some humans. And the visitor was an old bear, and a sick bear as well. He stood almost as high as Thor, but he was so old that he was only half as broad across the chest, and his neck and head were grotesquely thin. The Indians have a name for him. *Kuyas Wapusk* they call him—the bear so old he is about to die. They let him go unharmed; other bears tolerate him and let him eat their meat if he chances along; the white man kills him.

This old bear was famished. His claws were gone; his hair was thin, and in some places his skin was naked, and he had barely more than red, hard gums to chew with. If he lived until autumn he would den up—for the last time. Perhaps death would come even sooner than that. If so, *Kuyas Wapusk* would know in time, and he would crawl off into some hidden cave or deep crevice in the rocks to breathe his last. For in all the Rocky Mountains, so far as Bruce or Langdon knew, there was not a man who had found the bones or body of a grizzly that had died a natural death!

And big, hunted Thor, torn by wound and pursued by man, seemed to understand that this would be the last real feast on earth for *Kuyas Wapusk*—too old to fish for himself, too old to hunt, too old even to dig out the tender lily roots; and so he let him eat until the last fish was gone, and then went on, with Muskwa tagging at his heels.

CHAPTER
TWELVE

FOR still another two hours Thor led Muskwa on that tiresome jaunt into the north. They had traveled a good twenty miles since leaving the Bighorn Highway, and to the little tan-faced cub those twenty miles were like a journey around the world. Ordinarily he would not have gone that far away from his birthplace until his second year, and very possibly his third.

Not once in this hike down the valley had Thor wasted time on the mountain slopes. He had picked out the easiest trails along the creek. Three or four miles below the pool where they had left the old bear he suddenly changed this procedure by swinging due westward, and a little later they were once more climbing a mountain. They went up a long green slide for a quarter of a mile, and luckily for Muskwa's legs this brought them to the smooth plainlike floor of a break which took them without much more effort out on the slopes of the other valley. This was the valley in which Thor had killed the black bear twenty miles to the southward.

From the moment Thor looked out over the northern limits of his range a change took possession of him. All at once he lost his eagerness to hurry. For fifteen minutes he stood looking down into the valley, sniffing the air. He descended slowly, and when he reached the green meadows and the creek-bottom he mooshed along straight in the face of the wind, which was coming from the south and west. It did not bring him the scent he wanted—the smell of his mate. Yet an instinct that was more infallible than reason told him that she was near, or should be near. He did not take accident or sickness or the possibility of hunters having killed her into consideration. This was where he had always started in to hunt for her, and sooner or later he had found her. He knew her smell. And he crossed and recrossed the bottoms so that it could not escape him.

When Thor was lovesick he was more or less like a man: that is to say, he was an idiot. The importance of all other things dwindled into nothingness. His habits, which were as fixed as the stars at other times, took a complete vacation. He even forgot hunger, and the whistlers and gophers were quite safe. He was tireless. He rambled during the night as well as the day in quest of his ladylove.

It was quite natural that in these exciting hours he should forget Muskwa almost entirely. At least ten times before sunset he crossed and recrossed the creek, and the disgusted and almost ready-to-quit cub waded and swam and floundered after him until he was nearly drowned. The tenth or dozenth time Thor forded the stream Muskwa revolted and followed along on his own side. It was not long before the grizzly returned.

It was soon after this, just as the sun was setting, that the unexpected happened. What little wind there was suddenly swung straight into the east, and from the western slopes half a mile away it brought a scent that held Thor motionless in his tracks for perhaps half a minute, and then set him off on that ambling run which is the ungainliest gait of all four-footed creatures.

Muskwa rolled after him like a ball, pegging away for dear life, but losing ground at every jump. In that half-mile stretch he would have lost Thor altogether if the grizzly had not stopped near the bottom of the first slope to take fresh reckonings. When he started up the slope Muskwa could see him, and with a yelping cry for him to wait a minute set after him again.

Two or three hundred yards up the mountainside the slope shelved downward into a hollow, or dip, and nosing about in this dip, questing the air as Thor had quested it, was the beautiful she-grizzly from over the range. With her was one of her last year's cubs. Thor was within fifty yards of her when he came over the crest. He stopped. He looked at her. And Iskwao, "the female," looked at him.

Then followed true bear courtship. All haste, all eagerness, all desire for his mate seemed to have left Thor; and if Iskwao had been eager and yearning she was profoundly indifferent now. For two or three minutes Thor stood looking casually about, and this gave Muskwa time to come up and perch himself beside him, expecting another fight.

As though Thor was a thousand miles or so from her thoughts, Iskwao turned over a flat rock and began hunting for grubs and ants, and not to be outdone in this stoic unconcern Thor pulled up a bunch of grass and swallowed it. Iskwao moved a step or two, and Thor moved a step or two, and as if purely by accident their steps were toward each other.

Muskwa was puzzled. The older cub was puzzled. They sat on their haunches like two dogs, one three times as big as the other, and wondered what was going to happen.

It took Thor and Iskwao five minutes to arrive within five feet of each other, and then very decorously they smelled noses.

The year-old cub joined the family circle. He was of just the right age to have an exceedingly long name, for the Indians called him Pipoonaskoos, "the yearling." He came boldly up to Thor and his mother. For a moment Thor did not seem to notice him. Then his long right arm shot out in a sudden swinging uppercut that lifted Pipoonaskoos clean off the ground and sent him spinning two-thirds of the distance up to Muskwa.

The mother paid no attention to this elimination of her offspring, and still lovingly smelled noses with Thor. Muskwa, however, thought this was the preliminary of another tremendous fight, and with a yelp of defiance he darted down the slope and set upon Pipoonaskoos with all his might.

Pipoonaskoos was "mother's boy." That is, he was

one of those cubs who persist in following their mothers through a second season, instead of striking out for themselves. He had nursed until he was five months old; his parent had continued to hunt tidbits for him; he was fat, and sleek, and soft; he was, in fact, a "Willie" of the mountains.

On the other hand, a few days had put a lot of real mettle into Muskwa, and though he was only a third as large as Pipoonaskoos, and his feet were sore, and his back ached, he landed on the other cub like a shot out of a gun.

Still dazed by the blow of Thor's paw, Pipoonaskoos gave a yelping call to his mother for help at this sudden onslaught. He had never been in a fight, and he rolled over on his back and side, kicking and scratching and yelping as Muskwa's needlelike teeth sank again and again into his tender hide.

Luckily Muskwa got him once by the nose, and bit deep, and if there was any sand at all in Willie Pipoonaskoos this took it out of him, and while Muskwa held on for dear life he let out a steady stream of yelps, informing his mother that he was being murdered. To these cries Iskwao paid no attention at all, but continued to smell noses with Thor.

Finally freeing his bleeding nose, Pipoonaskoos shook Muskwa off by sheer force of superior weight and took to flight on a dead run. Muskwa pegged valiantly after him. Twice they made the circle of the basin, and in spite of his shorter legs, Muskwa was a close second in the race when Pipoonaskoos, turning an affrighted glance sidewise for an instant, hit against a rock and went sprawling. In another moment

Muskwa was at him again, and he would have continued biting and snarling until there was no more
strength left in him had he not happened to see Thor
and Iskwao disappearing slowly over the edge of the
slope toward the valley.

Almost immediately Muskwa forgot fighting. He
was amazed to find that Thor, instead of tearing up
the other bear, was walking off with her. Pipoonaskoos also pulled himself together and looked. Then
Muskwa looked at Pipoonaskoos, and Pipoonaskoos
looked at Muskwa. The tan-faced cub licked his chops
just once, as if torn between the prospective delight
of mauling Pipoonaskoos and the more imperative
duty of following Thor. The other gave him no choice.
With a whimpering yelp he set off after his mother.

Exciting times followed for the two cubs. All that
night Thor and Iskwao kept by themselves in the buffalo willow thickets and the balsams of the creek-
bottom. Early in the evening Pipoonaskoos sneaked
up to his mother again, and Thor lifted him into the
middle of the creek. The second visual proof of Thor's
displeasure impinged upon Muskwa the fact that the
older bears were not in a mood to tolerate the companionship of cubs, and the result was a wary and
suspicious truce between him and Pipoonaskoos.

All the next day Thor and Iskwao kept to themselves. Early in the morning Muskwa began adven-
turing about a little in quest of food. He liked tender
grass, but it was not very filling. Several times he saw
Pipoonaskoos digging in the soft bottom close to the
creek, and finally he drove the other cub away from
a partly dug hole and investigated for himself. After

a little more excavating he pulled out a white, bulbous, tender root that he thought was the sweetest and nicest thing he had ever eaten, not even excepting fish. It was the one *bonne bouche* of all the good things he would eventually learn to eat—the spring beauty. One other thing alone was at all comparable with it, and that was the dogtooth violet. Spring beauties were growing about him abundantly, and he continued to dig until his feet were grievously tender. But he had the satisfaction of being comfortably fed.

Thor was again responsible for a fight between Muskwa and Pipoonaskoos. Late in the afternoon the older bears were lying down side by side in a thicket when, without any apparent reason at all, Thor opened his huge jaws and emitted a low, steady, growling roar that sounded very much like the sound he had made when tearing the life out of the big black. Iskwao raised her head and joined him in the tumult, both of them perfectly good-natured and quite happy during the operation. Why mating bears indulge in this bloodcurdling duet is a mystery which only the bears themselves can explain. It lasts for about a minute, and during this particular minute Muskwa, who lay outside the thicket, thought that surely the glorious hour had come when Thor was beating up the parent of Pipoonaskoos. And instantly he looked for Pipoonaskoos.

Unfortunately the Willie-bear came sneaking round the edge of the brush just then, and Muskwa gave him no chance to ask questions. He shot at him in a black streak and Pipoonaskoos bowled over like a fat baby. For several minutes they bit and dug and clawed, most of the biting and digging and clawing being done by Muskwa, while Pipoonaskoos devoted his time and energy to yelping.

Finally the larger cub got away and again took to flight. Muskwa pursued him, into the brush and out, down to the creek and back, halfway up the slope and down again, until he was so tired he had to drop on his belly for a rest.

At this juncture Thor emerged from the thicket. He was alone. For the first time since last night he seemed to notice Muskwa. Then he sniffed the wind up the valley and down the valley, and after that turned and walked straight toward the distant slopes down which they had come the preceding afternoon. Muskwa was both pleased and perplexed. He wanted to go into the thicket and snarl and pull at the hide of the dead bear that must be in there, and he also wanted to finish Pipoonaskoos. After a moment or two of hesitation he ran after Thor and again followed close at his heels.

After a little Iskwao came from the thicket and nosed the wind as Thor had felt it. Then she turned in the opposite direction and, with Pipoonaskoos close behind her, went up the slope and continued slowly and steadily in the face of the setting sun.

So ended Thor's lovemaking and Muskwa's first fighting; and together they trailed eastward again, to face the most terrible peril that had ever come into the mountains for four-footed beast—a peril that was merciless, a peril from which there was no escape, a peril that was fraught with death.

CHAPTER
THIRTEEN

THE first night after leaving Iskwao and Pi-poonaskoos the big grizzly and the tan-faced cub wandered without sleep under the brilliant stars. Thor did not hunt for meat. He climbed a steep slope, then went down the shale side of a dip, and in a small basin hidden at the foot of a mountain came to a soft green meadow where the dogtooth violet, with its slender stem, its two lilylike leaves, its single cluster of five-petaled flowers, and its luscious, bulbous root, grew in great profusion. And here all through the night he dug and ate.

Muskwa, who had filled himself on spring beauty roots, was not hungry, and as the day had been a restful one for him, outside of his fighting, he found this night filled with its brilliant stars quite enjoyable. The moon came up about ten o'clock, and it was the biggest, and the reddest, and the most beautiful moon Muskwa had seen in his short life. It rolled up over the peaks like a forest fire, and filled all the Rocky Mountains with a wonderful glow. The basin, in which there were perhaps ten acres of meadow, was lighted up almost like day. The little lake at the foot of the mountain glimmered softly, and the tiny stream that fed it from the melting snows a thousand feet above shot down in glistening cascades that caught the moonlight like rivulets of dull polished diamonds.

About the meadow were scattered little clumps of bushes and a few balsams and spruce, as if set there for ornamental purposes; and on one side there was a narrow, verdure-covered slide that sloped upward for a third of a mile, and at the top of which, unseen by Muskwa and Thor, a band of sheep were sleeping.

Muskwa wandered about, always near Thor, investigating the clumps of bushes, the dark shadows of the balsams and spruce, and the edge of the lake. Here he found a plashet of soft mud which was a great solace to his sore feet. Twenty times during the night he waded in the mud.

Even when the dawn came Thor seemed to be in no great haste to leave the basin. Until the sun was well up he continued to wander about the meadow and the edge of the lake, digging up occasional roots, and eating tender grass. This did not displease Muskwa, who made his breakfast of the dogtooth violet bulbs. The one matter that puzzled him was why Thor did not go into the lake and throw out trout, for he yet had to learn that all water did not contain fish. At last he went fishing for himself, and succeeded in getting a black hard-shelled water beetle that nipped his nose with a pair of needlelike pincers and brought a yelp from him.

It was perhaps ten o'clock, and the sun-filled basin

was like a warm oven to a thick-coated bear, when Thor searched up among the rocks near the waterfall until he found a place that was as cool as an old-fashioned cellar. It was a miniature cavern. All about it the slate and sandstone was of a dark and clammy wet from a hundred little trickles of snow water that ran down from the peaks.

It was just the sort of a place Thor loved on a July day, but to Muskwa it was dark and gloomy and not a thousandth part as pleasant as the sun. So after an hour or two he left Thor in his frigidarium and began to investigate the treacherous ledges.

For a few minutes all went well—then he stepped on a green-tinted slope of slate over which a very shallow dribble of water was running. The water had been running over it in just that way for some centuries, and the shelving slate was worn as smooth as the surface of a polished pearl, and it was as slippery as a greased pole. Muskwa's feet went out from under him so quickly that he hardly knew what had happened. The next moment he was on his way to the lake a hundred feet below. He rolled over and over. He plashed into shallow pools. He was blinded and dazed by water and shock, and he gathered fresh speed with every yard he made. He had succeeded in letting out half a dozen terrified yelps at the start, and these roused Thor.

Where the water from the peaks fell into the lake there was a precipitous drop of ten feet, and over this Muskwa shot with a momentum that carried him twice as far out into the pond. He hit with a big splash, and disappeared. Down and down he went, where everything was black and cold and suffocating; then the life-preserver with which nature had endowed him in the form of his fat brought him to the surface. He began to paddle with all four feet. It was his first swim, and when he finally dragged himself ashore he was limp and exhausted.

While he still lay panting and very much frightened, Thor came down from the rocks. Muskwa's mother had given him a sound cuffing when he got the porcupine quill in his foot. She had cuffed him for every accident he had had, because she believed that cuffing was good medicine. Education is largely cuffed into a bear cub, and she would have given him a fine cuffing now. But Thor only smelled of him, saw that he was all right, and began to dig up a dogtooth violet.

He had not finished the violet when suddenly he stopped. For a half-minute he stood like a statue. Muskwa jumped and shook himself. Then he listened. A sound came to both of them. In one slow, graceful movement the grizzly reared himself to his full height. He faced the north, his ears thrust forward, the sensitive muscles of his nostrils twitching. He could smell nothing, but he *heard*!

Over the slopes which they had climbed there had come to him faintly a sound that was new to him, a sound that had never before been a part of his life. It was the barking of dogs.

For two minutes Thor sat on his haunches without moving a muscle of his great body except those twitching thews in his nose.

Deep down in this cup under the mountain it was difficult even for sound to reach him. Quickly he swung down on all fours and made for the green slope to the southward, at the top of which the band of sheep had slept during the preceding night. Muskwa hurried after.

A hundred yards up the slope Thor stopped and turned. Again he reared himself. Now Muskwa also faced to the north. A sudden downward drift of the wind brought the barking of the dogs to them clearly.

Less than half a mile away Langdon's pack of trained Airedales were hot on the scent. Their baying was filled with the fierce excitement which told Bruce and Langdon, a quarter of a mile behind them, that they were close upon their prey.

And even more than it thrilled them did the tonguing of the dogs thrill Thor. Again it was instinct that told him a new enemy had come into his world. He was not afraid. But that instinct urged him to retreat, and he went higher until he came to a part of the mountain that was rough and broken, where once more he halted.

This time he waited. Whatever the menace was it was drawing nearer with the swiftness of the wind. He could hear it coming up the slope that sheltered the basin from the valley.

The crest of that slope was just about on a level with Thor's eyes, and as he looked the leader of the pack came up over the edge of it and stood for a moment outlined against the sky. The others followed quickly, and for perhaps thirty seconds they stood rigid on the cap of the hill, looking down into the basin at their feet and sniffing the heavy scent with which it was filled.

During those thirty seconds Thor watched his enemies without moving, while in his deep chest there gathered slowly a low and terrible growl. Not until the pack swept down into the cup of the mountain, giving full tongue again, did he continue his retreat. But it was not flight. He was not afraid. He was going on—because to go on was his business. He was not seeking trouble; he had no desire even to defend his possession of the meadow and the little lake under the mountain. There were other meadows and other lakes, and he was not naturally a lover of fighting. But he was ready to fight.

He continued to rumble ominously, and in him there was burning a slow and sullen anger. He buried himself among the rocks; he followed a ledge with Muskwa slinking close at his heels; he climbed over a huge scarp of rock, and twisted among boulders half as big as houses. But not once did he go where Muskwa could not easily follow. Once, when he drew himself from a ledge to a projecting seam of sandstone higher up, and found that Muskwa could not climb it, he came down and went another way.

The baying of the dogs was now deep down in the basin. Then it began to rise swiftly, as if on wings, and Thor knew that the pack was coming up the green slide. He stopped again, and this time the wind brought their scent to him full and strong. It was a scent that tightened every muscle in his great body and set strange fires burning in him like raging furnaces. With the dogs came also the *man-smell*!

He traveled upward a little faster now, and the

fierce and joyous yelping of the dogs seemed scarcely a hundred yards away when he entered a small open space in the wild upheaval of rock. On the mountainside was a wall that rose perpendicularly. Twenty feet on the other side was a sheer fall of a hundred feet, and the way ahead was closed with the exception of a trail scarcely wider than Thor's body by a huge crag of rock that had fallen from the shoulder of the mountain. The big grizzly led Muskwa close up to this crag and the break that opened through it, and then turned suddenly back, so that Muskwa was behind him. In the face of the peril that was almost upon them a mother-bear would have driven Muskwa into the safety of a crevice in the rock wall. Thor did not do this. He fronted the danger that was coming, and reared himself up on his hind quarters.

Twenty feet away the trail he had followed swung sharply around a projecting bulge in the perpendicular wall, and with eyes that were now red and terrible Thor watched the trap he had set.

The pack was coming full tongue. Fifty yards beyond the bulge the dogs were running shoulder to shoulder, and a moment later the first of them rushed into the arena which Thor had chosen for himself. The bulk of the horde followed so closely that the first dogs were flung under him as they strove frantically to stop themselves in time.

With a roar Thor launched himself among them. His great right arm swept out and inward, and it seemed to Muskwa that he had gathered a half of the pack under his huge body. With a single crunch of his jaws he broke the back of the foremost hunter. From a second he tore the head so that the windpipe trailed out like a red rope.

He rolled himself forward, and before the remaining dogs could recover from their panic he had caught one a blow that sent him flying over the edge of the precipice to the rocks a hundred feet below. It had all happened in half a minute, and in that half-minute the remaining nine dogs had scattered.

But Langdon's Airedales were fighters. To the last dog they had come of fighting stock, and Bruce and Metoosin had trained them until they could be hung up by their ears without whimpering. The tragic fate of three of their number frightened them no more than their own pursuit had frightened Thor.

Swift as lightning they circled about the grizzly, spreading themselves on their forefeet, ready to spring aside or backward to avoid sudden rushes, and giving voice now to that quick, fierce yapping which tells hunters their quarry is at bay. This was their business—to harass and torment, to retard flight, to stop their prey again and again until their masters came to finish the kill. It was a quite fair and thrilling sport for the bear and the dogs. The man who comes up with the rifle ends it in murder.

But if the dogs had their tricks, Thor also had his. After three or four vain rushes, in which the Airedales eluded him by their superior quickness, he backed slowly toward the huge rock beside which Muskwa was crouching, and as he retreated the dogs advanced.

Their increased barking and Thor's evident inability to drive them away or tear them to pieces terrified Muskwa more than ever. Suddenly he turned tail and darted into a crevice in the rock behind him.

Thor continued to back until his great hips touched the stone. Then he swung his head sidewise and looked for the cub. Not a hair of Muskwa was to be seen. Twice Thor turned his head. After that, seeing that Muskwa was gone, he continued to retreat until he blocked the narrow passage that was his back door to safety.

The dogs were now barking like mad. They were drooling at their mouths, their wiry crests stood up like brushes, and their snarling fangs were bared to their red gums.

Nearer and nearer they came to him, challenging him to stay, to rush them, to catch them if he could— and in their excitement they put ten yards of open space behind them. Thor measured this space, as he had measured the distance between him and the young bull caribou a few days before. And then, without so much as a snarl of warning, he darted out upon his enemies with a suddenness that sent them flying wildly for their lives.

Thor did not stop. He kept on. Where the rock wall bulged out the trail narrowed to five feet, and he had measured this fact as well as the distance. He caught the last dog, and drove it down under his paw. As it was torn to pieces the Airedale emitted piercing cries of agony that reached Bruce and Langdon as they hurried panting and wind-broken up the slide that led from the basin.

Thor dropped on his belly in the narrowed trail, and as the pack broke loose with fresh voice he continued to tear at his victim until the rock was smeared with blood and hair and entrails. Then he rose to his feet and looked again for Muskwa. The cub was curled up in a shivering ball two feet in the crevice. It may be that Thor thought he had gone on up the mountain, for he lost no time now in retreating from the scene of battle. He had caught the wind again. Bruce and Langdon were sweating, and their smell came to him strongly.

For ten minutes Thor paid no attention to the eight dogs yapping at his heels, except to pause now and then and swing his head about. As he continued in his retreat the Airedales became bolder, until finally one of them sprang ahead of the rest and buried his fangs in the grizzly's leg.

This accomplished what barking had failed to do. With another roar Thor turned and pursued the pack headlong for fifty yards over the backtrail, and five precious minutes were lost before he continued upward toward the shoulder of the mountain.

Had the wind been in another direction the pack would have triumphed, but each time that Langdon and Bruce gained ground the wind warned Thor by bringing to him the warm odor of their bodies. And the grizzly was careful to keep that wind from the right quarter. He could have gained the top of the mountain more easily and quickly by quartering the face of it on a backtrail, but this would have thrown the wind too far under him. As long as he held the wind he was safe, unless the hunters made an effort to checkmate his method of escape by detouring and cutting him off.

It took him half an hour to reach the topmost ridge of rock, from which point he would have to break cover and reveal himself as he made the last two or three hundred yards up the shale side of the mountain to the backbone of the range.

When Thor made this break he put on a sudden spurt of speed that left the dogs thirty or forty yards behind him. For two or three minutes he was clearly outlined on the face of the mountain, and during the last minute of those three he was splendidly profiled against a carpet of pure-white snow, without a shrub or a rock to conceal him from the eyes below.

Bruce and Langdon saw him at five hundred yards, and began firing. Close over his head Thor heard the curious ripping wail of the first bullet, and an instant later came the crack of the rifle.

A second shot sent up a spurt of snow five yards ahead of him. He swung sharply to the right. This put him broadside to the marksmen. Thor heard a third shot—and that was all.

While the reports were still echoing among the crags and peaks something struck Thor a terrific blow on the flat of his skull, five inches back of his right ear. It was as if a club had descended upon him from out of the sky. He went down like a log.

It was a glancing shot. It scarcely drew blood, but for a moment it stunned the grizzly, as a man is dazed by a blow on the end of the chin.

Before he could rise from where he had fallen the dogs were upon him, tearing at his throat and neck and body. With a roar Thor sprang to his feet and shook them off. He struck out savagely, and Langdon and Bruce could hear his bellowing as they stood with fingers on the triggers of their rifles waiting for the dogs to draw away far enough to give them the final shots.

Yard by yard Thor worked his way upward, snarling at the frantic pack, defying the man-smell, the strange thunder, the burning lightning—even death itself, and five hundred yards below Langdon cursed despairingly as the dogs hung so close he could not fire.

Up to the very skyline the blood-thirsting pack shielded Thor. He disappeared over the summit. The dogs followed. And after that their baying came fainter and fainter as the big grizzly led them swiftly away from the menace of man in a long and thrilling race from which more than one was doomed not to return.

CHAPTER
FOURTEEN

IN HIS hiding-place Muskwa heard the last sounds of the battle on the ledge. The crevice was a V-shaped crack in the rock, and he had wedged himself as far back in this as he could. He saw Thor pass the opening of his refuge after he had killed the fourth dog; he heard the click, click, click of his claws as he retreated up the trail; and at last he knew that the grizzly was gone, and that the enemy had followed him.

Still he was afraid to come out. These strange pursuers that had come up out of the valley had filled him with a deadly terror. Pipoonaskoos had not made him afraid. Even the big black bear that Thor killed had not terrified him as these red-lipped, white-fanged strangers had frightened him. So he remained in his crevice, crowded as far back as he could get, like a wad shoved in a gun barrel.

He could still hear the tonguing of the dogs when other and nearer sounds alarmed him. Langdon and Bruce came rushing around the bulge in the mountain wall, and at the sight of the dead dogs they stopped. Langdon cried out in horror.

He was not more than twenty feet from Muskwa. For the first time the cub heard human voices; for the first time the sweaty odor of men filled his nostrils, and he scarcely breathed in his new fear. Then one of the hunters stood directly in front of the crack in which he was hidden, and he saw his first man. A moment later the men, too, were gone.

Later Muskwa heard the shots. After that the barking of the dogs grew more and more distant until finally he could not hear them at all. It was about three o'clock—the siesta hour in the mountains, and it was very quiet.

For a long time Muskwa did not move. He listened. And he heard nothing. Another fear was growing in him now—the fear of losing Thor. With every breath he drew he was hoping that Thor would return. For an hour he remained wedged in the rock. Then he heard a *cheep, cheep, cheep,* and a tiny striped rock-rabbit came out on the ledge where Muskwa could see him and began cautiously investigating one of the slain Airedales.

This gave Muskwa courage. He pricked up his ears a bit. He whimpered softly, as if beseeching recognition and friendship of the one tiny creature that was near him in this dreadful hour of loneliness and fear.

Inch by inch he crawled out of his hiding-place. At last his little round, furry head was out, and he looked about him. The trail was clear, and he advanced toward the rock-rabbit. With a shrill chatter the striped mite darted for its own stronghold, and Muskwa was alone again.

For a few moments he stood undecided, sniffing the air that was heavy with the scent of blood, of man, and of Thor; then he turned up the mountain.

He knew Thor had gone in that direction, and if little Muskwa possessed a mind and a soul they were filled with but one desire now—to overtake his big friend and protector. Even fear of dogs and men, unknown quantities in his life until today, was now overshadowed by the fear that he had lost Thor.

He did not need eyes to follow the trail. It was warm under his nose, and he started in the zigzag ascent of the mountain as fast as he could go. There were places where progress was difficult for his short legs, but he kept on valiantly and hopefully, encouraged by Thor's fresh scent.

It took him a good hour to reach the beginning of the naked shale that reached up to the belt of snow and the skyline, and it was four o'clock when he started up those last three hundred yards between him and the mountaintop. Up there he believed he would find Thor. But he was afraid, and he continued to whimper softly to himself as he dug his little claws bravely into the shale.

Muskwa did not look up to the crest of the peak again after he had started. To have done that it would have been necessary for him to stop and turn sidewise, for the ascent was steep. And so, when Muskwa was halfway to the top, it happened that he did not see Langdon and Bruce as they came over the skyline; and he could not smell them, for the wind was blowing up instead of down. Oblivious of their presence he came to the snowbelt. Joyously he smelled of Thor's huge footprints, and followed them. And above him Bruce and Langdon waited, crouched low, their guns on the ground, and each with his thick flannel shirt stripped off and held ready in his hands. When Muskwa was less than twenty yards from them they came tearing down upon him like an avalanche.

Not until Bruce was upon him did Muskwa recover himself sufficiently to move. He saw and realized danger in the last fifth of a second, and as Bruce flung himself forward, his shirt outspread like a net, Muskwa darted to one side. Sprawling on his face, Bruce gathered up a shirtful of snow and clutched it to his breast, believing for a moment that he had the cub, and at this same instant Langdon made a drive that entangled him with his friend's long legs and sent him turning somersaults down the snowslide.

Muskwa bolted down the mountain as fast as his short legs could carry him. In another second Bruce was after him, and Langdon joined in ten feet behind.

Suddenly Muskwa made a sharp turn, and the momentum with which Bruce was coming carried him thirty or forty feet below him, where the lanky mountaineer stopped himself only by doubling up like a jackknife and digging toes, hands, elbows, and even his shoulders into the soft shale.

Langdon had switched, and was hot after Muskwa. He flung himself face downward, shirt outspread, just as the cub made another turn, and when he rose to his feet his face was scratched and he spat half a handful of dirt and shale out of his mouth.

Unfortunately for Muskwa his second turn brought him straight down to Bruce, and before he could turn again he was enveloped in sudden darkness and suffocation, and over him there rang out a fiendish and triumphant yell.

"I got 'im!" shouted Bruce.

Inside the shirt Muskwa scratched and bit and snarled, and Bruce was having his hands full when Langdon ran down with the second shirt. Very shortly Muskwa was trussed up like a papoose. His legs and his body were swathed so tightly that he could not move them. His head was not covered. It was the only part of him that showed, and the only part of him that he could move, and it looked so round and frightened and funny that for a minute or two Langdon and Bruce forgot their disappointment and losses of the day and laughed.

Then Langdon sat down on one side of Muskwa, and Bruce on the other, and they filled and lighted their pipes. Muskwa could not even kick an objection.

"A couple of husky hunters we are," said Langdon then. "Come out for a grizzly and end up with that!"

He looked at the cub. Muskwa was eyeing him so earnestly that Langdon sat in mute wonder for a moment, and then slowly took his pipe from his mouth and stretched out a hand.

"Cubby, cubby, nice cubby," he cajoled softly.

Muskwa's tiny ears were perked forward. His bright eyes were like glass. Bruce, unobserved by Langdon, was grinning expectantly.

"Cubby won't bite—no—no—nice little cubby—we won't hurt cubby—"

The next instant a wild yell startled the mountain-tops as Muskwa's needlelike teeth sank into one of Langdon's fingers. Bruce's howls of joy would have frightened game a mile away.

"You little devil!" gasped Langdon, and then, as he sucked his wounded finger, he laughed with Bruce. "He's a sport—a dead game sport," he added. "We'll call him Spitfire, Bruce. By George, I've wanted a cub like that ever since I first came into the mountains. I'm going to take him home with me! Ain't he a funny-looking little cuss?"

Muskwa shifted his head, the only part of him that was not as stiffly immovable as a mummy, and scrutinized Bruce. Langdon rose to his feet and looked back to the skyline. His face was set and hard.

"Four dogs!" he said, as if speaking to himself. "Three down below—and one up there!" He was silent for a moment, and then said: "I can't understand it, Bruce. They've cornered fifty bears for us, and until today we've never lost a dog."

Bruce was looping a buckskin thong about Muskwa's middle, making of it a sort of handle by which he could carry the cub as he would have conveyed a pail of water or a slab of bacon. He stood up, and Muskwa dangled at the end of his string.

"We've run up against a killer," he said. "An' a meat-killin' grizzly is the worst animal on the face of the earth when it comes to a fight or a hunt. The dogs'll never hold 'im, Jimmy, an' if it don't get dark pretty soon there won't none of the bunch come back. They'll quit at dark—if there's any left. The old fellow's got our wind, an' you can bet he knows what knocked

138

him down up there on the snow. He's hikin'—an' hikin' fast. When we see 'im ag'in it'll be twenty miles from here."

Langdon went up for the guns. When he returned Bruce led the way down the mountain, carrying Muskwa by the buckskin thong. For a few moments they paused on the bloodstained ledge of rock where Thor had wreaked his vengeance upon his tormentors. Langdon bent over the dog the grizzly had decapitated.

"This is Biscuits," he said. "And we always thought she was the one coward of the bunch. The other two are Jane and Tober; old Fritz is up on the summit. Three of the best dogs we had, Bruce!"

Bruce was looking over the ledge. He pointed downward.

"There's another—pitched clean off the face o' the mount'in!" he gasped. "Jimmy, that's five!"

Langdon's fists were clenched tightly as he stared over the edge of the precipice. A choking sound came from his throat. Bruce understood its meaning. From where they stood they could see a black patch on the upturned breast of the dog a hundred feet under them. Only one of the pack was marked like that. It was Langdon's favorite. He had made her a camp pet.

"It's Dixie," he said. For the first time he felt a surge of anger sweep through him, and his face was white as he turned back to the trail. "I've got more than one reason for getting that grizzly now, Bruce," he added. "Wild horses can't tear me away from these mountains until I kill him. I'll stick until winter if I have to. I swear I'm going to kill him—if he doesn't run away."

"He won't do that," said Bruce tersely, as he once more swung down the trail with Muskwa.

Until now Muskwa had been stunned into submissiveness by what must have appeared to him to be an utterly hopeless situation. He had strained every muscle in his body to move a leg or a paw, but he was swathed as tightly as Ramses had ever been. But now, however, it slowly dawned upon him that as he dangled back and forth his face frequently brushed his enemy's leg, and he still had the use of his teeth. He watched his opportunity, and this came when Bruce took a long step down from a rock, thus allowing Muskwa's body to rest for the fraction of a second on the surface of the stone from which he was descending.

Quicker than a wink Muskwa took a bite. It was a good deep bite, and if Langdon's howl had stirred the silences a mile away the yell which now came from Bruce beat him by at least a half. It was the wildest, most bloodcurdling sound Muskwa had ever heard, even more terrible than the barking of the dogs, and it frightened him so that he released his hold at once.

Then, again, he was amazed. These queer bipeds made no effort to retaliate. The one he had bitten hopped up and down on one foot in a most unaccountable manner for a minute or so, while the other sat down on a boulder and rocked back and forth, with his hands on his stomach, and made a queer, uproarious noise with his mouth wide open. Then the other stopped his hopping and also made that queer noise.

It was anything but laughter to Muskwa. But it impinged upon him the truth of one of two things: either these grotesque-looking monsters did not dare to fight him, or they were very peaceful and had no intention of harming him. But they were more cautious thereafter, and as soon as they reached the valley they carried him between them, strung on a rifle barrel.

It was almost dark when they approached a clump of balsams red with the glow of a fire. It was Muskwa's first fire. Also he saw his first horses, terrific-looking monsters even larger than Thor.

A third man—Metoosin, the Indian—came out to meet the hunters, and into this creature's hands Muskwa found himself transferred. He was laid on his side with the glare of the fire in his eyes, and while one of his captors held him by both ears, and so tightly that it hurt, another fastened a hobblestrap around his neck for a collar. A heavy halter rope was then tied to the ring on this strap, and the end of the rope was fastened to a tree.

During these operations Muskwa snarled and snapped as much as he could. In another half-minute he was free of the shirts, and as he staggered on four wobbly legs, from which all power of flight had temporarily gone, he bared his tiny fangs and snarled as fiercely as he could.

To his further amazement this had no effect upon his strange company at all, except that the three of them—even the Indian—opened their mouths and joined in that loud and incomprehensible din, to which one of them had given voice when he sank his teeth into his captor's leg on the mountainside. It was all tremendously puzzling to Muskwa.

CHAPTER
FIFTEEN

GREATLY to Muskwa's relief the three men soon turned away from him and began to busy themselves about the fire. This gave him a chance to escape, and he pulled and tugged at the end of the rope until he nearly choked himself to death. Finally he gave up in despair, and crumpling himself up against the foot of the balsam he began to watch the camp.

He was not more than thirty feet from the fire. Bruce was washing his hands in a canvas basin, Langdon was mopping his face with a towel. Close to the fire Metoosin was kneeling, and from the big black skittle he was holding over the coals came the hissing and sputtering of fat caribou steaks, and about the pleasantest smell that had ever come Muskwa's way. The air all about him was heavy with the aroma of good things.

When Langdon had finished drying his face he opened a can of something. It was sweetened condensed milk. He poured the white fluid into a basin, and came with it toward Muskwa. The cub had unsuccessfully attempted flight on the ground until his neck was sore; now he climbed the tree. He went up so quickly that Langdon was astonished, and he snarled and spat at the man as the basin of milk was placed where he would almost fall into it when he came down.

Muskwa remained at the end of his rope up the tree, and for a long time the hunters paid no more attention to him. He could see them eating and he could hear them talking as they planned a new campaign against Thor.

"We've got to trick him after what happened today," declared Bruce. "No more tracking 'im after this, Jimmy. We can track until doomsday an' he'll always know where we are." He paused for a moment and listened. "Funny the dogs don't come," he said. "I wonder—"

He looked at Langdon.

"Impossible!" exclaimed the latter, as he read the significance of his companion's look. "Bruce, you don't mean to say that bear might kill them all!"

"I've hunted a good many grizzlies," replied the mountaineer quietly, "but I ain't never hunted a trickier one than this. Jimmy, he trapped them dogs on the ledge, an' he tricked the dog he killed up on the peak. He's liable to get 'em all into a corner, an' if that happens—"

He shrugged his shoulders suggestively.

Again Langdon listened.

"If there were any alive at dark they should be

here pretty soon," he said. "I'm sorry, now—sorry we didn't leave the dogs at home."

Bruce laughed a little grimly.

"Fortunes o' war, Jimmy," he said. "You don't go hunting grizzlies with a pack of lapdogs, an' you've got to expect to lose some of them sooner or later. We've tackled the wrong bear, that's all. He's beat us."

"Beat us?"

"I mean he's beat us in a square game, an' we dealt a raw hand at that in using dogs at all. Do you want that bear bad enough to go after him my way?"

Langdon nodded.

"What's your scheme?"

"You've got to drop pretty ideas when you go grizzly-hunting," began Bruce. "And especially when you run up against a 'killer.' There won't be any hour between now an' denning-up time that this grizzly doesn't get the wind from all directions. How? He'll make detours. I'll bet if there was snow on the ground you'd find him backtracking two miles out of every six, so he can get the wind of anything that's following him. An' he'll travel mostly nights, layin' high up in the rocks an' shale during the day. If you want any more shootin', there's just two things to do, an' the best of them two things is to move on and find other bears."

"Which I won't do, Bruce. What's your scheme for getting this one?"

Bruce was silent for several moments before he replied.

"We've got his range mapped out to a mile," he said then. "It begins up at the first break we crossed, an' it ends down here where we came into this valley. It's about twenty-five miles up an' down. He don't touch the mount'ins west of this valley nor the mount'ins east of the other valley, an' he's dead certain to keep on makin' circles so long as we're after him. He's hikin' southward now on the other side of the range.

"We'll lay here for a few days an' not move. Then we'll start Metoosin through the valley over there with the dogs, if there's any left, and we'll start south through this valley at the same time. One of us will keep to the slopes an' the other to the bottom, an' we'll travel slow. Get the idea?

"That grizzly won't leave his country, an' Metoosin is pretty near bound to drive him around to us. We'll let him do the open hunting an' we'll skulk. The bear can't get past us both without giving one of us shooting."

"It sounds good," agreed Langdon. "And I've got a lame knee that I'm not unwilling to nurse for a few days."

Scarcely were the words out of Langdon's mouth when a sudden rattle of hobblechains and the startled snort of a grazing horse out in the meadow brought them both to their feet.

"Utim!" whispered Metoosin, his dark face aglow in the firelight.

"You're right—the dogs," said Bruce, and he whistled softly.

They heard a movement in the brush near them, and a moment later two of the dogs came into the firelight. They slunk in, half on their bellies, and as they prostrated themselves at the hunters' feet a third and a fourth joined them.

They were not like the pack that had gone out that morning. There were deep hollows in their sides; their wiry crests were flat; they were hard run, and they knew that they were beaten. Their aggressiveness was gone, and they had the appearance of whipped curs.

A fifth came in out of the night. He was limping, and dragging a torn foreleg. The head and throat of one of the others was red with blood. They all lay flat on their bellies, as if expecting condemnation.

"We have failed," their attitude said; "we are beaten, and this is all of us that are left."

Mutely Bruce and Langdon stared at them. They listened—waited. No other came. And then they looked at each other.

"Two more of them gone," said Langdon.

Bruce turned to a pile of panniers and canvases and pulled out the dog leashes. Up in his tree Muskwa was all atremble. Within a few yards of him he saw again the white-fanged horde that had chased Thor and had driven him into the rock-crevice. Of the men he was no longer greatly afraid. They had attempted him no harm, and he had ceased to quake and snarl when one of them passed near. But the dogs were monsters. They had given battle to Thor. They must have beaten him, for Thor had run away.

The tree to which Muskwa was fastened was not much more than a sapling, and he lay in the saddle of a crotch five feet from the ground when Metoosin led one of the dogs past him. The Airedale saw him and made a sudden spring that tore the leash from the Indian's hand. His leap carried him almost up to Muskwa. He was about to make another spring when Langdon rushed forward with a fierce cry, caught the dog by his collar, and with the end of the leash gave him a sound beating. Then he led him away.

This act puzzled Muskwa more than ever. The man had saved him. He had beaten the monster with the red mouth and the white fangs, and all of those monsters were now being taken away at the end of ropes.

When Langdon returned he stopped close to Muskwa's tree and talked to him. Muskwa allowed Langdon's hand to approach within six inches of him, and did not snap at it. Then a strange and sudden thrill shot through him. While his head was turned a little Langdon had boldly put his hand on his furry back. And in the touch there was not hurt! His mother had never put her paw on him as gently as that!

Half a dozen times in the next ten minutes Langdon touched him. For the first three or four times Muskwa bared his two rows of shining teeth, but he made no sound. Gradually he ceased even to bare his teeth.

Langdon left him then, and in a few moments he returned with a chunk of raw caribou meat. He held this close to Muskwa's nose. Muskwa could smell it, but he backed away from it, and at last Langdon placed it beside the basin at the foot of the tree and returned to where Bruce was smoking.

"Inside of two days he'll be eating out of my hand," he said.

It was not long before the camp became very quiet.

Langdon, Bruce, and the Indian rolled themselves in their blankets and were soon asleep. The fire burned lower and lower. Soon there was only a single smoldering log. An owl hooted a little deeper in the timber. The drone of the valley and the mountains filled the peaceful night. The stars grew brighter. Far away Muskwa heard the rumbling of a boulder rolling down the side of a mountain.

There was nothing to fear now. Everything was still and asleep but himself, and very cautiously he began to back down the tree. He reached the foot of it, loosed his hold, and half fell into the basin of condensed milk, a part of it slopping up over his face. Involuntarily he shot out his tongue and licked his chops, and the sweet, sticky stuff that it gathered filled him with a sudden and entirely unexpected pleasure. For a quarter of an hour he licked himself. And then, as if the secret of this delightful ambrosia had just dawned upon him, his bright little eyes fixed themselves covetously upon the tin basin. He approached it with commendable strategy and caution, circling first on one side of it and then on the other, every muscle in his body prepared for a quick spring backward if it should make a jump for him. At last his nose touched the thick, luscious feast in the basin, and he did not raise his head again until the last drop of it was gone.

The condensed milk was the one biggest factor in the civilizing of Muskwa. It was the missing link that connected certain things in his lively little mind. He knew that the same hand that had touched him so gently had also placed this strange and wonderful feast at the foot of his tree, and that same hand had also offered him meat. He did not eat the meat, but he licked the interior of the basin until it shone like a mirror in the starlight.

In spite of the milk, he was still filled with a desire to escape, though his efforts were not as frantic and unreasoning as they had been. Experience had taught him that it was futile to jump and tug at the end of his leash, and now he fell to chewing at the rope. Had he gnawed in one place he would probably have won freedom before morning, but when his jaws became tired he rested, and when he resumed his work it was usually at a fresh place in the rope. By midnight his gums were sore, and he gave up his exertions entirely.

Humped close to the tree, ready to climb up it at the first sign of danger, the cub waited for morning. Not a wink did he sleep. Even though he was less afraid than he had been, he was terribly lonesome. He missed Thor, and he whimpered so softly that the men a few yards away could not have heard him had they been awake. If Pipoonaskoos had come into the camp then he would have welcomed him joyfully.

Morning came, and Metoosin was the first out of his blankets. He built a fire, and this roused Bruce and Langdon. The latter, after he had dressed himself, paid a visit to Muskwa, and when he found the basin licked clean he showed his pleasure by calling the others' attention to what had happened.

Muskwa had climbed to his crotch in the tree, and again he tolerated the stroking touch of Langdon's hand. Then Langdon brought forth another can from a cowhide pannier and opened it directly under Muskwa, so that he could see the creamy white fluid as it was turned into the basin. He held the basin up to Muskwa, so close that the milk touched the cub's nose, and for the life of him Muskwa could not keep his tongue in his mouth. Inside of five minutes he was eating from the basin in Langdon's hand! But when Bruce came up to watch the proceedings the cub bared all his teeth and snarled.

"Bears make better pets than dogs," affirmed Bruce a little later, when they were eating breakfast. "He'll be following you around like a puppy in a few days, Jimmy."

"I'm getting fond of the little cuss already," replied Langdon. "What was that you were telling me about Jameson's bears, Bruce?"

"Jameson lived up in the Kootenay country," said Bruce. "Reg'lar hermit, I guess you'd call him. Came out of the mountains only twice a year to get grub. He made pets of grizzlies. For years he had one as big as this fellow we're chasing. He got 'im when a cub, an' when I saw him he weighed a thousand pounds an' followed Jameson wherever he went like a dog. Even went on his hunts with him, an' they slept beside the same campfire. Jameson loved bears, an' he'd never kill one."

Langdon was silent. After a moment he said:

"And I'm beginning to love them, Bruce. I don't know just why, but there's something about bears that makes you love them. I'm not going to shoot many more—perhaps none after we get this dog-killer we're after. I almost believe he will be my last bear." Suddenly he clenched his hands, and added angrily: "And to think there isn't a province in the Dominion or a state south of the Border that has a 'closed season' for bear! It's an outrage, Bruce. They're classed with vermin, and can be exterminated at all seasons. They can even be dug out of their dens with their young— and—so help me Heaven!—I've helped to dig them out! We're beasts, Bruce. Sometimes I almost think it's a crime for a man to carry a gun. And yet—I go on killing."

"It's in our blood," laughed Bruce, unmoved. "Did you ever know a man, Jimmy, that didn't like to see things die? Wouldn't every mother's soul of 'em go to a hanging if they had the chance? Won't they crowd like buzzards round a dead horse to get a look at a man crushed to a pulp under a rock or a locomotive engine? Why, Jimmie, if there weren't no law to be afraid of, we humans'd be killing one another for the fun of it! We would. It's born in us to want to kill."

"And we take it all out on brute creation," mused Langdon. "After all, we can't have much sympathy for ourselves if a generation or two of us are killed in war, can we? Mebby you're right, Bruce. Inasmuch as we can't kill our neighbors legally whenever we have the inclination, it's possible the Chief Arbiter of things sends us a war now and then to relieve us temporarily of our bloodthirstiness. Hello, what in thunder is the cub up to now?"

Muskwa had fallen the wrong way out of his crotch and was dangling like the victim at the end of a hangman's rope. Langdon ran to him, caught him boldly in his bare hands, lifted him up over the limb and placed him on the ground. Muskwa did not snap at him or even growl.

Bruce and Metoosin were away from camp all of that day, spying over the range to the westward, and Langdon was left to doctor a knee which he had battered against a rock the previous day. He spent most of his time in company with Muskwa. He opened a can of their griddle-cake syrup and by noon he had the cub following him about the tree and straining to reach the dish which he held temptingly just out of reach. Then he would sit down, and Muskwa would climb half over his lap to reach the syrup.

At his present age Muskwa's affection and confidence were easily won. A baby black bear is very much like a human baby: he likes milk, he loves sweet things, and he wants to cuddle up close to any living thing that is good to him. He is the most lovable creature on four legs—round and soft and fluffy, and so funny that he is sure to keep every one about him in good humour. More than once that day Langdon laughed until the tears came, and especially when Muskwa made determined efforts to climb up his leg to reach the dish of syrup.

As for Muskwa, he had gone syrup mad. He could not remember that his mother had ever given him anything like it, and Thor had produced nothing better than fish.

Late in the afternoon Langdon untied Muskwa's rope and led him for a stroll down toward the creek. He carried the syrup dish and every few yards he would pause and let the cub have a taste of its contents. After half an hour of this maneuvering he dropped his end of the leash entirely, and walked campward. And Muskwa followed! It was a triumph, and in Langdon's veins there pulsed a pleasurable thrill which his life in the open had never brought to him before.

It was late when Metoosin returned, and he was quite surprised that Bruce had not shown up. Darkness came, and they built up the fire. They were finishing supper an hour later when Bruce came in, carrying something swung over his shoulders. He tossed it close to where Muskwa was hidden behind his tree.

"A skin like velvet, and some meat for the dogs," he said. "I shot it with my pistol."

He sat down and began eating. After a little Muskwa cautiously approached the carcass that lay doubled up three or four feet from him. He smelled of it, and a curious thrill shot through him. Then he whimpered softly as he muzzled the soft fur, still warm with life. And for a time after that he was very still.

For the thing that Bruce had brought into camp and flung at the foot of his tree was the dead body of little Pipoonaskoos!

CHAPTER
SIXTEEN

THAT night the big loneliness returned to Muskwa. Bruce and Metoosin were so tired after their hard climb over the range that they went to bed early, and Langdon followed them, leaving Pipoonaskoos where Bruce had first thrown him.

Scarcely a move had Muskwa made after the discovery that had set his heart beating a little faster. He did not know what death was, or what it meant, and as Pipoonaskoos was so warm and soft he was sure that he would move after a little. He had no inclination to fight him now.

Again it grew very, very still, and the stars filled the sky, and the fire burned low. But Pipoonaskoos did not move. Gently at first, Muskwa began nosing him and pulling at his silken hair, and as he did this he whimpered softly, as if saying, "I don't want to fight you any more, Pipoonaskoos! Wake up, and let's be friends!"

But still Pipoonaskoos did not stir, and at last

Muskwa gave up all hope of waking him. And still whimpering to his fat little enemy of the green meadow how sorry he was that he had chased him, he snuggled close up to Pipoonaskoos and in time went to sleep.

Langdon was first up in the morning, and when he came over to see how Muskwa had fared during the night he suddenly stopped, and for a full minute he stood without moving, and then a low, strange cry broke from his lips. For Muskwa and Pipoonaskoos were snuggled as closely as they could have snuggled had both been living, and in some way Muskwa had arranged it so that one of the dead cub's little paws was embracing him.

Quietly Langdon returned to where Bruce was sleeping, and in a minute or two Bruce returned with him, rubbing his eyes. And then he, too, stared, and the men looked at each other.

"Dog meat," breathed Langdon. "You brought it home for dog meat, Bruce!"

Bruce did not answer, Langdon said nothing more, and neither talked very much for a full hour after that. During that hour Metoosin came and dragged Pipoonaskoos away, and instead of being skinned and fed to the dogs he was put into a hole down in the creek-bottom and covered with sand and stones. That much, at least, Bruce and Langdon did for Pipoonaskoos.

This day Metoosin and Bruce again went over the range. The mountaineer had brought back with him bits of quartz in which were unmistakable signs of gold, and they returned with an outfit for panning.

Langdon continued his education of Muskwa. Several times he took the cub near the dogs, and when they snarled and strained at the ends of their leashes he whipped them, until with quick understanding they gripped the fact that Muskwa, although a bear, must not be harmed.

In the afternoon of this second day he freed the cub entirely from the rope, and he had no difficulty in recapturing it when he wanted to tie it up again. The third and fourth days Bruce and the Indian explored the valley west of the range and convinced themselves finally that the "colors" they found were only a part of the flood-drifts, and would not lead to fortune.

On this fourth night, which happened to be thick with clouds, and chilly, Langdon experimented by taking Muskwa to bed with him. He expected trouble. But Muskwa was as quiet as a kitten, and once he found a proper nest for himself he scarcely made a move until morning. A part of the night Langdon slept with one of his hands resting on the cub's soft, warm body.

According to Bruce it was now time to continue the hunt for Thor, but a change for the worse in Langdon's knee broke in upon their plans. It was impossible for Langdon to walk more than a quarter of a mile at a time, and the position he was compelled to take in the saddle caused him so much pain that to prosecute the hunt even on horseback was out of the question.

"A few more days won't hurt any," consoled Bruce. "If we give the old fellow a longer rest he may get a bit careless."

The three days that followed were not without profit and pleasure for Langdon. Muskwa was teaching him more than he had ever known about bears, and especially bear cubs, and he made notes voluminously.

The dogs were now confined to a clump of trees fully three hundred yards from the camp, and gradually the cub was given his freedom. He made no effort to run away, and he soon discovered that Bruce and Metoosin were also his friends. But Langdon was the only one he would follow.

On the morning of the eighth day after their pursuit of Thor, Bruce and Metoosin rode over into the eastward valley with the dogs. Metoosin was to have a day's start, and Bruce planned to return to camp that afternoon so that he and Langdon could begin their hunt up the valley the next day.

It was a glorious morning. A cool breeze came from the north and west, and about nine o'clock Langdon fastened Muskwa to his tree, saddled a horse, and rode down the valley. He had no intention of hunting. It was a joy merely to ride and breathe in the face of that wind and gaze upon the wonders of the mountains.

He traveled northward for three or four miles, until he came to a broad, low slope that broke through the range to the westward. A desire seized upon him to look over into the other valley, and as his knee was giving him no trouble he cut a zigzag course upward that in half an hour brought him almost to the top.

Here he came to a short, steep slide that compelled him to dismount and continue on foot. At the summit he found himself on a level sweep of meadow, shut in on each side of him by the bare rock walls of the split mountains, and a quarter of a mile ahead he could see where the meadow broke suddenly into the slope that shelved downward into the valley he was seeking.

Halfway over this quarter of a mile of meadow there was a dip into which he could not see, and as he came to the edge of this he flung himself suddenly upon his face and for a minute or two lay as motionless as a rock. Then he slowly raised his head.

A hundred yards from him, gathered about a small waterhole in the hollow, was a herd of goats. There were thirty or more, most of them nannies with young kids. Langdon could make out only two billies in the lot. For half an hour he lay still and watched them. Then one of the nannies struck out with her two kids for the side of the mountain; another followed, and seeing that the whole band was about to move, Langdon rose quickly to his feet and ran as fast as he could toward them.

For a moment nannies, billies, and little kids were paralyzed by his sudden appearance. They faced half about and stood as if without the power of flight until he had covered half the distance between them. Then their wits seemed to return all at once, and they broke in a wild panic for the side of the nearest mountain. Their hoofs soon began to clatter on boulder and shale, and for another half-hour Langdon heard the hollow booming of the rocks loosened by their feet high up among the crags and peaks. At the end of that time they were infinitesimal white dots on the skyline.

He went on, and a few minutes later looked down into the other valley. Southward this valley was shut out from his vision by a huge shoulder of rock. It was not very high, and he began to climb it. He had almost reached the top when his toe caught in a piece of slate, and in falling he brought his rifle down with tremendous force on a boulder.

He was not hurt, except for a slight twinge in his lame knee. But his gun was a wreck. The stock was shattered close to the breech and a twist of his hand broke it off entirely.

As he carried two extra rifles in his outfit the mishap did not disturb Langdon as much as it might otherwise have done, and he continued to climb over the rocks until he came to what appeared to be a broad, smooth ledge leading around the sandstone spur of the mountain. A hundred feet farther on he found the ledge ended in a perpendicular wall of rock. From this point, however, he had a splendid view of the broad sweep of country between the two ranges to the south. He sat down, pulled out his pipe, and prepared to enjoy the magnificent panorama under him while he was getting his wind.

Through his glasses he could see for miles, and what he looked upon was an unhunted country. Scarcely half a mile away a band of caribou was filing slowly across the bottom toward the green slopes to the west. He caught the glint of many ptarmigan wings in the sunlight below. After a time, fully two miles away, he saw sheep grazing on a thinly verdured slide.

He wondered how many valleys there were like this in the vast reaches of the Canadian mountains that stretched three hundred miles from sea to prairie and a thousand miles north and south. Hundreds, even thousands, he told himself, and each wonderful valley a world complete within itself; a world filled with its own life, its own lakes and streams and forests, its own joys and its own tragedies.

Here in this valley into which he gazed was the same soft droning and the same warm sunshine that had filled all the other valleys; and yet here, also, was a different life. Other bears ranged the slopes that he could see dimly with his naked eyes far to the west and north. It was a new domain, filled with other promise and other mystery, and he forgot time and hunger as he sat lost in the enchantment of it.

It seemed to Langdon that these hundreds or thousands of valleys would never grow old for him; that he could wander on for all time, passing from one into another, and that each would possess its own charm, its own secrets to be solved, its own life to be learned. To him they were largely inscrutable; they were cryptic, as enigmatical as life itself, hiding their treasures as they droned through the centuries, giving birth to multitudes of the living, demanding in return other multitudes of the dead. As he looked off through the sunlit space he wondered what the story of this valley would be, and how many volumes it would fill, if the valley itself could tell it.

First of all, he knew, it would whisper of the creation of a world; it would tell of oceans torn and twisted and thrown aside—of those first strange aeons of time when there was no night, but all was day; when weird and tremendous monsters stalked where he now saw the caribou drinking at the creek, and when huge winged creatures half bird and half beast swept the sky where he now saw an eagle soaring.

And then it would tell of The Change—of that terrific hour when the earth tilted on its axis, and night came, and a tropical world was turned into a frigid one, and new kinds of life were born to fill it.

It must have been long after that, thought Langdon, that the first bear came to replace the mammoth, the mastodon, and the monstrous beasts that had been their company. And that first bear was the forefather of the grizzly he and Bruce were setting forth to kill the next day!

So engrossed was Langdon in his thoughts that he did not hear a sound behind him. And then something roused him.

It was as if one of the monsters he had been picturing in his imagination had let out a great breath close to him. He turned slowly, and the next moment his heart seemed to stop its beating; his blood seemed to grow cold and lifeless in his veins.

Barring the ledge not more than fifteen feet from

him, his great jaws agape, his head moving slowly from side to side as he regarded his trapped enemy, stood Thor, the King of the Mountains!

And in that space of a second or two Langdon's hands involuntarily gripped at his broken rifle, and he decided that he was doomed!

CHAPTER
SEVENTEEN

A BROKEN, choking breath—a stifled sound that was scarcely a cry—was all that came from Langdon's lips as he saw the monstrous grizzly looking at him. In the ten seconds that followed he lived hours.

His first thought was that he was powerless—utterly powerless. He could not even run, for the rock wall was behind him; he could not fling himself valleyward, for there was a sheer fall of a hundred feet on that side. He was face to face with death, a death as terrible as that which had overtaken the dogs.

And yet in these last moments Langdon did not lose himself in terror. He noted even the redness of the avenging grizzly's eyes. He saw the naked scar along his back where one of his bullets had plowed; he saw the bare spot where another of his bullets had torn its way through Thor's fore-shoulder. And he believed, as he observed these things, that Thor had deliberately trailed him, that the bear had followed him along the ledge and had cornered him here that he might repay in full measure what had been inflicted upon him.

Thor advanced—just one step; and then, in that slow, graceful movement, reared himself to full height. Langdon, even then, thought that he was magnificent. On his part, the man did not move; he looked steadily up at Thor, and he had made up his mind what to do when the great beast lunged forward. He would fling himself over the edge. Down below there was one chance in a thousand for life. There might be a ledge or a projecting spur to catch him.

And Thor!

Suddenly—unexpectedly—he had come upon man! This was the creature that had hunted him, this was the creature that had hurt him—and it was so near that he could reach out with his paw and crush it! And how weak, and white, and shrinking it looked now! Where was its strange thunder? Where was its burning lightning? Why did it make no sound?

Even a dog would have done more than this creature, for the dog would have shown its fangs; it would have snarled, it would have fought. But this thing that was man did nothing. And a great, slow doubt swept through Thor's massive head. Was it really this shrinking, harmless, terrified thing that had hurt him? He smelled the man-smell. It was thick. And yet this time there came with it no hurt.

And then, slowly again, Thor came down to all fours. Steadily he looked at the man.

Had Langdon moved then he would have died. But Thor was not, like man, a murderer. For another half-minute he waited for a hurt, for some sign of menace.

Neither came, and he was puzzled. His nose swept the ground, and Langdon saw the dust rise where the grizzly's hot breath stirred it. And after that, for another long and terrible thirty seconds, the bear and the man looked at each other.

Then very slowly—and doubtfully—Thor half turned. He growled. His lips drew partly back. Yet he saw no reason to fight, for that shrinking, white-faced pigmy crouching on the rock made no movement to offer him battle. He saw that he could not go on, for the ledge was blocked by the mountain wall. Had there been a trail the story might have been different for Langdon. As it was, Thor disappeared slowly in the direction from which he had come, his great head hung low, his long claws click, click, clicking like ivory castanets as he went.

Not until then did it seem to Langdon that he breathed again, and that his heart resumed its beating. He gave a great sobbing gasp. He rose to his feet, and his legs seemed weak. He waited—one minute, two, three; and then he stole cautiously to the twist in the ledge around which Thor had gone.

The rocks were clear, and he began to retrace his own steps toward the meadowy break, watching and listening, and still clutching the broken parts of his rifle. When he came to the edge of the plain he dropped down behind a huge boulder.

Three hundred yards away Thor was ambling slowly over the crest of the dip toward the eastward valley. Not until the bear reappeared on the farther ridge of the hollow, and then vanished again, did Langdon follow.

When he reached the slope on which he had hobbled his horse Thor was no longer in sight. The horse was where he had left it. Not until he was in the saddle did Langdon feel that he was completely safe. Then he laughed, a nervous, broken, joyous sort of laugh, and as he scanned the valley he filled his pipe with fresh tobacco.

"You great big god of a bear!" he whispered, and every fiber in him was trembling in a wonderful excitement as he found voice for the first time. "You— you monster with a heart bigger than man!" And then he added, under his breath, as if not conscious that he was speaking: "If I'd cornered you like that I'd have killed you! And you! You cornered me, and let me live!"

He rode toward camp, and as he went he knew that this day had given the final touch to the big change that had been working in him. He had met the King of the Mountains; he had stood face to face with death, and in the last moment the four-footed thing he had hunted and maimed had been merciful. He believed that Bruce would not understand; that Bruce could not understand; but unto himself the day and the hour had brought its meaning in a way that he would not forget so long as he lived, and he knew that hereafter and for all time he would not again hunt the life of Thor, or the lives of any of his kind.

Langdon reached the camp and prepared himself some dinner, and as he ate this, with Muskwa for company, he made new plans for the days and weeks that were to follow. He would send Bruce back to overtake Metoosin the next day, and they would no longer hunt the big grizzly. They would go on to the Skeena and possibly even up to the edge of the Yukon, and then swing eastward into the caribou country sometime early in September, hitting back toward civilization on the prairie side of the Rockies. He would take Muskwa with them. Back in the land of men and cities they would be great friends. It did not occur to him just then what this would mean for Muskwa.

It was two o'clock, and he was still dreaming of new and unknown trails into the North when a sound came to rouse and disturb him. For a few minutes he paid no attention to it, for it seemed to be only a part of the droning murmur of the valley. But slowly and steadily it rose above this, and at last he got up from where he was lying with his back to a tree and walked out from the timber, where he could hear more plainly.

Muskwa followed him, and when Langdon stopped the tan-faced cub also stopped. His little ears shot out inquisitively. He turned his head to the north. From that direction the sound was coming.

In another moment Langdon had recognized it, and yet even then he told himself that his ears must be playing him false. It could not be the barking of dogs! By this time Bruce and Metoosin were far to the south with the pack; at least Metoosin should be, and Bruce was on his return to the camp! Quickly the sound grew more distinct, and at last he knew that he could not be mistaken. The dogs were coming up the valley. Something had turned Bruce and Metoosin northward instead of into the south. And the pack was giving tongue—that fierce, heated baying which told him they were again on the fresh spoor of game. A sudden thrill shot through him. There could be but one living thing in the length and breadth of the valley that Bruce would set the dogs after, and that was the big grizzly!

For a few moments longer Langdon stood and listened. Then he hurried back to camp, tied Muskwa to his tree, armed himself with another rifle, and resaddled his horse. Five minutes later he was riding swiftly in the direction of the range where a short time before Thor had given him his life.

CHAPTER
EIGHTEEN

THOR heard the dogs when they were a mile away. There were two reasons why he was even less in a mood to run from them now than a few days before. Of the dogs alone he had no more fear than if they had been so many badgers, or so many whistlers piping at him from the rocks. He had found them all mouth and little fang, and easy to kill. It was what followed close after them that disturbed him. But today he had stood face to face with the thing that had brought the strange scent into his valleys, and it had not offered to hurt him, and he had refused to kill it. Besides, he was again seeking Iskwao, the she-bear, and man is not the only animal that will risk his life for love.

After killing his last dog at dusk of that fatal day when they had pursued him over the mountain Thor had done just what Bruce thought that he would do, and instead of continuing southward had made a wider detour toward the north, and the third night after the fight and the loss of Muskwa he found Iskwao again. In the twilight of that same evening Pipoonaskoos had died, and Thor had heard the sharp cracking of Bruce's automatic. All that night and the next day and the night that followed he spent with Iskwao, and then he left her once more. A third time he was seeking her when he found Langdon in the trap on the ledge, and he had not yet got wind of her when he first heard the baying of the dogs on his trail.

He was traveling southward, which brought him nearer the hunters' camp. He was keeping to the high slopes where there were little dips and meadows, broken by patches of shale, deep coulees, and occasionally wild upheavals of rock. He was keeping the wind straight ahead so that he would not fail to catch the smell of Iskwao when he came near her, and with the baying of the dogs he caught no scent of the pursuing beasts, or of the two men who were riding behind them.

At another time he would have played his favorite trick of detouring so that the danger would be ahead of him, with the wind in his favor. Caution had now become secondary to his desire to find his mate. The dogs were less than half a mile away when he stopped suddenly, sniffed the air for a moment, and then went on swiftly until he was halted by a narrow ravine.

Up that ravine Iskwao was coming from a dip lower down the mountain, and she was running. The yelping of the pack was fierce and close when Thor scrambled down in time to meet her as she rushed upward. Iskwao paused for a single moment, smelled noses with Thor, and then went on, her ears laid back flat and sullen and her throat filled with growling menace.

Thor followed her, and he also growled. He knew that his mate was fleeing from the dogs, and again that deadly and slowly increasing wrath swept through him as he climbed after her higher up the mountain.

In such an hour as this Thor was at his worst. He was a fighter when pursued as the dogs had pursued him a week before—but he was a demon, terrible and without mercy, when danger threatened his mate.

He fell farther and farther behind Iskwao, and twice he turned, his fangs gleaming under drawn lips, and his defiance rolling back upon his enemies in low thunder.

When he came up out of the coulee he was in the shadow of the peak, and Iskwao had already disappeared in her skyward scramble. Where she had gone was a wild chaos of rockslide and the piled-up debris of fallen and shattered masses of sandstone crag. The skyline was not more than three hundred yards above him. He looked up. Iskwao was among the rocks, and here was the place to fight. The dogs were close upon him now. They were coming up the last stretch of the coulee, baying loudly. Thor turned about, and waited for them.

Half a mile to the south, looking through his glasses, Langdon saw Thor, and at almost the same instant the dogs appeared over the edge of the coulee. He had ridden halfway up the mountain; from that point he had climbed higher, and was following a well-beaten sheep trail at about the same altitude as Thor. From where he stood the valley lay under his glasses for miles. He did not have far to look to discover

Bruce and the Indian. They were dismounting at the foot of the coulee, and as he gazed they ran quickly into it and disappeared.

Again Langdon swung back to Thor. The dogs were holding him now, and he knew there was no chance of the grizzly killing them in that open space. Then he saw movement among the rocks higher up, and a low cry of understanding broke from his lips as he made out Iskwao climbing steadily toward the ragged peak. He knew that this second bear was a female. The big grizzly—her mate—had stopped to fight. And there was no hope for him if the dogs succeeded in holding him for a matter of ten or fifteen minutes. Bruce and Metoosin would appear in that time over the rim of the coulee at a range of less than a hundred yards!

Langdon thrust his binoculars in their case and started at a run along the sheep trail. For two hundred yards his progress was easy, and then the patch broke into a thousand individual tracks on a slope of soft and slippery shale, and it took him five minutes to make the next fifty yards.

The trail hardened again. He ran on pantingly, and for another five minutes the shoulder of a ridge hid Thor and the dogs from him. When he came over that ridge and ran fifty yards, down the farther side of it, he stopped short. Further progress was barred by a steep ravine. He was five hundred yards from where Thor stood with his back to the rocks and his huge head to the pack.

Even as he looked, struggling to get breath enough to shout, Langdon expected to see Bruce and Metoosin appear out of the coulee. It flashed upon him then that even if he could make them hear it would be impossible for them to understand him. Bruce would not guess that he wanted to spare the beast they had been hunting for almost two weeks.

Thor had rushed the dogs a full twenty yards toward the coulee when Langdon dropped quickly behind a rock. There was only one way of saving him now, if he was not too late. The pack had retreated a few yards down the slope, and he aimed at the pack. One thought only filled his brain—he must sacrifice his dogs or let Thor die. And that day Thor had given him his life!

There was no hesitation as he pressed the trigger. It was a long shot, and the first bullet threw up a cloud of dust fifty feet short of the Airedales. He fired again, and missed. The third time his rifle cracked there answered it a sharp yelp of pain which Langdon himself did not hear. One of the dogs rolled over and over down the slope.

The reports of the shots alone had not stirred Thor, but now when he saw one of his enemies crumple up and go rolling down the mountain he turned slowly toward the safety of the rocks. A fourth and then a fifth shot followed, and at the fifth the yelping dogs dropped back toward the coulee, one of them limping with a shattered forefoot.

Langdon sprang upon the boulder over which he had rested his gun, and his eyes caught the skyline. Iskwao had just reached the top. She paused for a moment and looked down. Then she disappeared.

Thor was now hidden among the boulders and broken masses of sandstone, following her trail. Within two minutes after the grizzly disappeared Bruce and Metoosin scrambled up over the edge of the coulee. From where they stood even the skyline was within fairly good shooting distance, and Langdon suddenly began shouting excitedly, waving his arms, and pointing *downward*.

Bruce and Metoosin were caught by his ruse, in spite of the fact that the dogs were again giving fierce tongue close to the rocks among which Thor had gone. They believed that from where he stood Langdon could see the progress of the bear, and that it was running toward the valley. Not until they were another hundred yards down the slope did they stop and look back at Langdon to get further directions. From his rock Langdon was pointing to the skyline.

Thor was just going over. He paused for a moment, as Iskwao had stopped, and took one last look at man.

And Langdon, as he saw the last of him, waved his hat and shouted, "Good luck to you, old man—good luck!"

CHAPTER
NINETEEN

THAT night Langdon and Bruce made their new plans, while Metoosin sat aloof, smoking in stolid silence, and gazing now and then at Langdon as if he could not yet bring himself to the point of believing what had happened that afternoon. Thereafter through many moons Metoosin would never forget to relate to his children and his grandchildren and his friends of the tepee tribes how he had once hunted with a white man who had shot his own dogs to save the life of a grizzly bear. Langdon was no longer the same old Langdon to him, and after this hunt Metoosin knew that he would never hunt with him again. For Langdon was *keskwao* now. Something had gone wrong in his head. The Great Spirit had taken away his heart and had given it to a grizzly bear, and over his pipe Metoosin watched him cautiously. This suspicion was confirmed when he saw Bruce and Langdon making a cage out of a cowhide pannier and realized that the cub was to accompany them on their long journey. There was no doubt in his mind now. Langdon was "queer," and to an Indian that sort of queerness boded no good to man.

The next morning at sunrise the outfit was ready for its long trail into the northland. Bruce and Langdon led the way up the slope and over the divide into the valley where they had first encountered Thor, the train filing picturesquely behind them, with Metoosin bringing up the rear. In his cowhide pannier rode Muskwa.

Langdon was satisfied and happy.

"It was the best hunt of my life," he said to Bruce. "I'll never be sorry we let him live."

"You're the doctor," said Bruce rather irreverently. "If I had my way about it his hide would be back there on Dishpan. Almost any tourist down on the line of rail would jump for it at a hundred dollars."

"He's worth several thousand to me alive," replied Langdon, with which enigmatic retort he dropped behind to see how Muskwa was riding.

The cub was rolling and pitching about in his pannier like a raw amateur in a howdah on an elephant's back, and after contemplating him for a few moments Langdon caught up with Bruce again.

Half a dozen times during the next two or three hours he visited Muskwa, and each time that he returned to Bruce he was quieter, as if debating something with himself.

It was nine o'clock when they came to what was

undoubtedly the end of Thor's valley. A mountain rose up squarely in the face of it, and the stream they were following swung sharply to the westward into a narrow canyon. On the east rose a green and undulating slope up which the horses could easily travel, and which would take the outfit into a new valley in the direction of the Driftwood. This course Bruce decided to pursue.

Halfway up the slope they stopped to give the horses a breathing spell. In his cowhide prison Muskwa whimpered pleadingly. Langdon heard, but he seemed to pay no attention. He was looking steadily back into the valley. It was glorious in the morning sun. He could see the peaks under which lay the cool, dark lake in which Thor had fished; for miles the slopes were like green velvet, and there came to him as he looked the last droning music of Thor's world. It struck him in a curious way as a sort of anthem, a hymnal rejoicing that he was going, and that he was leaving things as they were before he came. And yet, *was* he leaving things as they had been? Did his ears not catch in that music of the mountains something of sadness, of grief, of plaintive prayer?

And again, close to him, Muskwa whimpered softly.

Then Langdon turned to Bruce.

"It's settled," he said, and his words had a decisive ring in them. "I've been trying to make up my mind all the morning, and it's made up now. You and Metoosin go on when the horses get their wind. I'm going to ride down there a mile or so and free the cub where he'll find his way back home!"

He did not wait for arguments or remarks, and Bruce made none. He took Muskwa in his arms and rode back into the south.

A mile up the valley Langdon came to a wide, open meadow dotted with clumps of spruce and willows and sweet with the perfume of flowers. Here he dismounted, and for ten minutes sat on the ground with Muskwa. From his pocket he drew forth a small paper bag and fed the cub its last sugar. A thick lump grew in his throat as Muskwa's soft little nose muzzled the palm of his hand, and when at last he jumped up and sprang into his saddle there was a mist in his eyes. He tried to laugh. Perhaps he was weak. But he loved Muskwa, and he knew that he was leaving more than a human friend in this mountain valley.

"Good-bye, old fellow," he said, and his voice was choking. "Good-bye, little Spitfire! Mebby some day I'll come back and see you, and you'll be a big, fierce bear—but I won't shoot—never— never—"

He rode fast into the north. Three hundred yards away he turned his head and looked back. Muskwa was following, but losing ground. Langdon waved his hand.

"Good-bye!" he called through the lump in his throat. "Good-bye!"

Half an hour later he looked down from the top of the slope through his glasses. He saw Muskwa, a black dot. The cub had stopped, and was waiting confidently for him to return.

And trying to laugh again, but failing dismally, Langdon rode over the divide and out of Muskwa's life.

CHAPTER
TWENTY

FOR a good half-mile Muskwa followed over the trail of Langdon. He ran at first; then he walked; finally he stopped entirely and sat down like a dog, facing the distant slope. Had Langdon been afoot he would not have halted until he was tired. But the cub had not liked his pannier prison. He had been tremendously jostled and bounced about, and twice the horse that carried him had shaken himself, and those shakings had been like earthquakes to Muskwa. He knew that the cage as well as Langdon was ahead of him. He sat for a time and whimpered wistfully, but he went no farther. He was sure that the friend he had grown to love would return after a little. He always came back. He had never failed him. So he began to hunt about for a spring beauty or a dogtooth violet, and for some time he was careful not to stray very far away from where the outfit had passed.

All that day the cub remained in the flower-strewn meadows under the slope; it was very pleasant in the sunshine, and he found more than one patch of the bulbous roots he liked. He dug, and he filled himself, and he took a nap in the afternoon; but when the sun began to go down and the heavy shadows of the mountain darkened the valley he began to grow afraid.

He was still a very small baby of a cub, and only that one dreadful night after his mother had died had he spent entirely alone. Thor had replaced mother, and Langdon had taken the place of Thor, so that until now he had never felt the loneliness and emptiness of darkness. He crawled under a clump of thorn close to the trail, and continued to wait, and listen, and sniff expectantly. The stars came out clear and brilliant, but tonight their lure was not strong enough to call him forth. Not until dawn did he steal out cautiously from his shelter of thorn.

The sun gave him courage and confidence again and he began wandering back through the valley, the scent of the horse-trail growing fainter and fainter until at last it disappeared entirely. That day Muskwa ate some grass and a few dogtooth violet roots, and when the second night came he was abreast of the slope over which the outfit had come from the valley in which were Thor and Iskwao. He was tired and hungry, and he was utterly lost.

That night he slept in the end of a hollow log. The next day he went on, and for many days and many nights after that he was alone in the big valley. He passed close to the pool where Thor and he had met the old bear, and he nosed hungrily among the fish-bones; he skirted the edge of the dark, deep lake; he saw the shadowy things fluttering in the gloom of the forest again; he passed over the beaver dam, and he slept for two nights close to the logjam from which he had watched Thor throw out their first fish. He was almost forgetting Langdon now, and he was thinking more and more about Thor and his mother. He wanted them. He wanted them more than he had ever wanted the companionship of man, for Muskwa was fast becoming a creature of the wild again.

It was the beginning of August before the cub came to the break in the valley and climbed up over the slope where Thor had first heard the thunder and had first felt the sting of the white men's guns. In these two weeks Muskwa had grown rapidly, in spite of the fact that he often went to bed on an empty stomach; and he was no longer afraid of the dark. Through the deep, sunless canyon above the clay wallow he went, and as there was only one way out he came at last to the summit of the break over which Thor had gone, and over which Langdon and Bruce had followed in close pursuit. And the other valley—his home—lay under Muskwa.

Of course he did not recognize it. He saw and smelled in it nothing that was familiar. But it was such a beautiful valley, and so abundantly filled with plenty and sunshine, that he did not hurry through it. He found whole gardens of spring beauties and dogtooth violets. And on the third day he made his first real kill. He almost stumbled over a baby whistler no larger than a red squirrel, and before the little creature could escape he was upon it. It made him a splendid feast.

It was fully a week before he passed along the creek-bottom close under the slope where his mother had died. If he had been traveling along the crest of the slope he would have found her bones, picked clean by the wild things. It was another week before he came to the little meadow where Thor had killed the bull caribou and the big black bear.

And now Muskwa knew that he was home!

For two days he did not travel two hundred yards from the scene of feast and battle, and night and day he was on the watch for Thor. Then he had to seek farther for food, but each afternoon when the mountains began to throw out long shadows he would return to the clump of trees in which they had made the cache that the black bear robber had despoiled.

One day he went farther than usual in his quest for roots. He was a good half-mile from the place he had made home, and he was sniffing about the end of a rock when a great shadow fell suddenly upon him. He looked up, and for a full half-minute he stood transfixed, his heart pounding and jumping as it had never pounded and jumped before in his life. Within five feet of him stood Thor! The big grizzly was as motionless as he, looking at him steadily. And then Muskwa gave a puppylike whine of joy and ran forward. Thor lowered his huge head, and for another half-minute they stood without moving, with Thor's nose buried in the hair on Muskwa's back. After that Thor went up the slope as if the cub had never been lost at all, and Muskwa followed him happily.

Many days of wonderful travel and of glorious feasting came after this, and Thor led Muskwa into a thousand new places in the two valleys and the mountains between. There were great fishing days, and there was another caribou killed over the range, and Muskwa grew fatter and fatter and heavier and heavier until by the middle of September he was as large as a good-sized dog.

Then came the berries, and Thor knew where they all grew low down in the valleys—first the wild red raspberries, then the soap berries, and after those the delicious black currants which grew in the cool depths of the forests and were almost as large as cherries and nearly as sweet as the sugar which Langdon had fed Muskwa. Muskwa liked the black currants best of all. They grew in thick, rich clusters; there were no leaves on the bushes that were loaded with them, and he could pick and eat a quart in five minutes.

But at last the time came when there were no berries. This was in October. The nights were very cold, and for whole days at a time the sun would not shine, and the skies were dark and heavy with clouds. On the peaks the snow was growing deeper and deeper, and it never thawed now up near the skyline. Snow fell in the valley, too—at first just enough to make a white carpet that chilled Muskwa's feet, but it quickly disappeared. Raw winds began to come out of the north, and in place of the droning music of the valley in summertime there were now shrill wailings and screechings at night, and the trees made mournful sounds.

To Muskwa the whole world seemed changing. He wondered in these chill and dark days why Thor kept to the windswept slopes when he might have found shelter in the bottoms. And Thor, if he explained to him at all, told him that winter was very near, and that these slopes were their last feeding grounds. In the valleys the berries were gone; grass and roots alone were no longer nourishing enough for their bodies; they could no longer waste time in seeking ants and grubs; the fish were in deep water. It was the season when the caribou were keen-scented as foxes and swift as the wind. Only along the slopes lay the dinners they were sure of—famine-day dinners of whistlers and gophers. Thor dug for them now, and in this digging Muskwa helped as much as he could. More than once they turned out wagonloads of earth to get at the cozy winter sleeping quarters of a whistler family, and sometimes they dug for hours to capture three or four little gophers no larger than red squirrels, but lusciously fat.

Thus they lived through the last days of October into November. And now the snow and the cold winds and the fierce blizzards from the north came in earnest, and the ponds and lakes began to freeze over. Still Thor hung to the slopes, and Muskwa shivered with the cold at night and wondered if the sun was never going to shine again.

One day about the middle of November Thor stopped in the very act of digging out a family of whistlers, went straight down into the valley, and struck southward in a most businesslike way. They were ten miles from the clay-wallow canyon when they started, but so lively was the pace set by the big grizzly that they reached it before dark that same afternoon.

For two days after this Thor seemed to have no object in life at all. There was nothing in the canyon to eat, and he wandered about among the rocks, smelling and listening and deporting himself generally in a fashion that was altogether mystifying to Muskwa. In the afternoon of the second day Thor stopped in a clump of jackpines under which the ground was strewn with fallen needles. He began to eat these needles. They did not look good to Muskwa, but something told the cub that he should do as Thor was doing; so he licked them up and swallowed them, not knowing that it was nature's last preparation for his long sleep.

It was four o'clock when they came to the mouth of the deep cavern in which Thor was born, and here again Thor paused, sniffing up and down the wind, and waiting for nothing in particular.

It was growing dark. A wailing storm hung over the canyon. Biting winds swept down from the peaks, and the sky was black and full of snow.

For a minute the grizzly stood with his head and shoulders in the cavern door. Then he entered. Muskwa followed. Deep back they went through a pitch-black gloom, and it grew warmer and warmer, and the wailing of the wind died away until it was only a murmur.

It took Thor at least half an hour to arrange himself just as he wanted to sleep. Then Muskwa curled up beside him. The cub was very warm and very comfortable.

That night the storm raged, and the snow fell deep. It came up the canyon in clouds, and it drifted down through the canyon roof in still thicker clouds, and all the world was buried deep. When morning came there was no cavern door, there were no rocks, and no black and purple of tree and shrub. All was white and still, and there was no longer the droning music in the valley.

Deep back in the cavern Muskwa moved restlessly. Thor heaved a deep sigh. After that long and soundly they slept. And it may be that they dreamed.

James Oliver Curwood, 1923, Mounds Resort, Houghton Lake, Michigan (Photo contributed with the kind permission of Ivan A. Conger, of Owosso, Michigan, editor of *The Curwood Collector*)

About the Author

JAMES OLIVER CURWOOD (1878–1927) was one of America's most popular wilderness adventure writers and an early conservationist, fighting for ecology long before it became the popular movement of today. He wrote thirty-three books, including *The Grizzly King,* the 1916 novel on which the movie *The Bear* is based, and which has been reissued by Newmarket Press under the title *The Bear: A Novel.* The character of James Langdon in this novel mirrors Curwood's own experience in the Canadian wilderness.

After serving as a newspaper reporter in Detroit, Curwood traveled throughout Canada, exploring its untainted beauty. He built his own log cabins from British Columbia to northern Quebec, often spending six months out of the year in the wilds of the North, and then would return to his hometown of Owosso, Michigan, to write about his adventures.

Curwood was a longtime hunter of wild game, but as he grew older—and especially after his experience of coming face to face with a grizzly who chose not to kill him—he favored the camera over a rifle because of his ever-increasing respect for animal life. Curwood fought to preserve the wilderness along with its inhabitants, which were being destroyed at an alarming rate at the turn of the century.

In 1927 he was appointed Chairman of the Game, Fish, and Wildlife Committee of the Michigan Department of Conservation. He became well known for his outspoken views on preserving the delicate balance of nature.

Curwood's other books, many of which were also made into films, include *The River's End* (which sold over 100,000 copies), *The Valley of Silent Men, God's Country: The Trail to Happiness, Nomads of the North, Kazan, The Flaming Forest,* and *The Gold Hunters.* His books have been translated into many languages, including Chinese.

Curwood has enjoyed tremendous popularity. *The New York Times Book Review* of February 1918 states: "Curwood has an invaluable gift of the born narrator—the ability to tell a story and tell it in an interesting and vivid way." During his lifetime Curwood enjoyed international fame for his novels and was regarded by many readers as being in a class with Jack London and Zane Grey.

Curwood is survived by a granddaughter and two great-grandchildren. His home is maintained as a historic site in Owosso, where a Curwood Festival is held annually. In 1979 a James Oliver Curwood Literary Award of Shiawassee County was established for the best essays written on the subjects of conservation and ecology.

NEWMARKET MEDALLION EDITIONS FOR YOUNG READERS

As for these titles at your local bookstore, or order from: Newmarket Press, 18 East 48 Street, New York, NY 10017 (212) 832-3575

Dances With Wolves: The Illustrated Screenplay and Story Behind the Film
Kevin Costner, Michael Blake, and Jim Wilson
Here is the actual screenplay of the Academy Award–winning movie, 16 pages of behind-the-scenes stories, and over 40 pictures and drawings.
(144 pp; 5″ x 8″)
_____ Medallion paperback, $4.95

James Oliver Curwood

Baree, The Story of a Wolf-Dog
The third book in Curwood's Nature Series is a powerful adventure story about a half-wild wolf-pup separated from his parents in the Canadian wilderness, and the otters, rabbits, owls, bears, and other creatures he encounters there. "A timeless tale…Curwood captures the simplicity and beauty of nature."—*ALA Booklist*
(256 pp; 5″ x 8″)
_____ Medallion paperback, $3.95
_____ hardcover, $18.95

The Bear
The spectacular success of the movie triggered the rediscovery of this long-lost adventure story about Thor, a mighty grizzly, and Muskwa, a motherless bear cub, who travel from one adventure to another while two trappers draw nearer and nearer. "Spellbinding—as thrilling as the movie!"—*The Kirkus Reviews*
(208 pp; 5″ x 8″)
_____ Medallion paperback, $3.95
_____ hardcover, $16.95

For postage and handling add $2.00 for the first book, plus $1.00 for each additional book thereafter. Please allow 4 to 6 weeks for delivery. Prices and availability are subject to change.

I am enclosing a check or money order payable to NEWMARKET PRESS, in the amount of $_____ .

Name_____

Address_____

City/State_____

For quotes on special quantity purchase discounts, or for a copy of our catalog, please write or call the Newmarket Press Special Sales Department.

medallionbob.92

DANCES WITH WOLVES BOOKS FROM NEWMARKET PRESS

Newmarket Press is the official movie tie-in publisher for *Dances With Wolves*. Ask for these books at your local bookstore, or order from Newmarket Press, 18 East 48 Street, New York, NY 10017 (212) 832-3575

Dances With Wolves: The Illustrated Story of the Epic Film
Kevin Costner, Michael Blake, & Jim Wilson. Photos by Ben Glass.
The topselling illustrated moviebook of all time includes screenplay, production notes, the complete credit roll, editorial and art features on Native Americans, the frontier, the Civil War, and exclusive introductions by the authors.
(160 pp; 8⅜″ x 10⅞″; 170 photos and drawings, 80 in color)
_____ hardcover, $29.95
_____ large format paperback, $16.95

Dances With Wolves: The Illustrated Screenplay and Story Behind the Film
(digest version)
An abridged edition of the bestselling moviebook, this low-priced reprint includes the complete screenplay, 16 pages of production notes, the credits, over 40 b&w photos and drawings. (144 pp.; 5³⁄₁₆″ x 8″)
_____ Medallion paperback, $4.95

Dances With Wolves: A Story for Children
Adapted by James Howe, based on the Michael Blake screenplay.
For all ages—a children's version of the now classic story of John Dunbar's life on the frontier among the Indians, illustrated with 68 color photos from the movie. (64 pp.; 8⅜″ x 10⅞″)
_____ hardcover (jacketed), $14.95

Dances With Wolves—The Novel
Michael Blake
The original novel that was the inspiration and basis for the award-winning movie, with a new afterword by the author. (336 pp; 5½″ x 8¼″)
_____ hardcover (jacketed), $18.95

For postage and handling add $2.00 for the first book, plus $1.00 for each additional book thereafter. Please allow 4 to 6 weeks for delivery. Prices and availability are subject to change.

I am enclosing a check or money order payable to NEWMARKET PRESS, in the amount of $_____ .

Name_____

Address_____

City/State_____

For quotes on special quantity purchase discounts, or for a copy of our catalog, please write or call the Newmarket Press Special Sales Department.